365

DAYS OF

Understanding

YOUR GRIEF

Companion
PRESS

*Companion Press is dedicated to the
education and support of both the bereaved
and bereavement caregivers. We believe that those
who companion the bereaved by walking with them
as they journey in grief have a wondrous opportunity:
to help others embrace and grow through grief—
and to lead fuller, more deeply-lived lives
themselves because of this important ministry.*

For a complete catalog and ordering
information, write, call, or visit:

Companion Press
The Center for Loss and Life Transition
3735 Broken Bow Road, Fort Collins, CO 80526
(970) 226-6050
www.centerforloss.com

ALSO BY DR. ALAN WOLFELT

Understanding Your Grief:
Ten Essential Touchstones for Finding Hope
and Healing Your Heart

Grief One Day at a Time:
365 Meditations to Help You Heal After Loss

The Understanding Your Grief Journal:
Exploring the Ten Essential Touchstones

One Mindful Day at a Time:
365 Meditations for Living in the Now

365
DAYS OF
Understanding
YOUR GRIEF

DAILY READINGS FOR
FINDING HOPE AND
HEALING YOUR HEART

ALAN D. WOLFELT, PH.D.

Companion Press is an imprint of the Center for Loss and Life Transition, 3735 Broken Bow Road, Fort Collins, Colorado 80526.

26 25 24 23   6 5 4

ISBN: 978-1-61722-299-3

For my precious first grandchild, Grayson

Welcome

After a significant loss, your grief is with you every day. You know this, and you're wise to turn to a source of daily support.

I wrote this little book to be your compassionate companion as you journey through the wilderness of your grief. I invite you to read each day's entry when you awaken each morning. It will help set the tone for your day and serve as a reminder that your grief, while painful, is a normal, necessary part of your love for the person who died. It will also provide you with the small doses of encouragement and hope you need and deserve.

I've been a grief counselor and educator for more than forty years, and it was nearly thirty years ago that I wrote the first edition of my flagship book for mourners, *Understanding Your Grief*. I'm humbled that it has gone on to help many thousands of people and is used in grief support groups across the globe. This daily version of *Understanding Your*

Grief parses the reading into tiny, digestible bits. At the same time, it also expands the content, adding a myriad of new ideas and guidance. You can read one without the other or both—together or sequentially.

In addition, this book encourages mindfulness. The practice of living in the now is so helpful for everyone but especially mourners because it gets us out of our heads and into our hearts. It encourages us to be with our feelings, to practice self-care, and to continue to turn our awareness to the miracles of each moment.

In that spirit, you'll see that this book includes a brief "reflection" on the bottom of every page. Over the years I've often been asked to give some direction for grievers who feel they've absorbed the teachings in *Understanding Your Grief* and want to continue befriending them. The reflections are intended to encourage you to journey all through your very unique and personal grief—to help you, when you are ready, gently embrace your need to openly and authentically mourn. Perhaps you can think of this book and these reflections as an invitation—an invitation to mourn.

THE 10 TOUCHSTONES FOR HEALING YOUR HEART

In the wilderness of your grief, the ten touchstones are the trail markers that let you know you are on the right path.

1

Open to the presence of your loss

2

Dispel the misconceptions about grief

3

Embrace the uniqueness of your grief

4

Explore your feelings of loss

Understand the six needs of mourning

Recognize you are not crazy

Nurture yourself

Reach out for help

Seek reconciliation, not resolution

Appreciate your transformation

THE 6 NEEDS OF MOURNING

The six needs of mourning are like their
own little grouping of trail markers.
These are the needs that all mourners
must accept and work on in order
to journey toward healing.

1 Acknowledge the reality of the death

2 Embrace the pain of the loss

3 Remember the person who died

4 Develop a new self-identity

5 Search for meaning

6 Let others help you—now and always

The content of this book originates from my own experiences with grief as well as my work companioning thousands of people who have experienced the death of someone loved. I realize that some of these daily entries may not speak to your unique journey. Some may even run counter to your experience. I urge you to take from this book only what is useful to you and ignore the rest.

I would, of course, hope that you find this book to be one way of caring for yourself during this difficult time. Self-care when we are grieving is essential to our survival. For it is in nurturing ourselves—in allowing ourselves the time and attention we need to befriend our grief—that we eventually find meaning and purpose in our continued living. My experience has taught me that it is in having the courage to care for our own needs that we discover that we can come out of the dark and into the light.

Thank you for allowing me to companion you on this difficult journey. And now, let's get started...

Alan D. Wolfelt

I resolve to mourn

That's it. That's really the only resolution
I need this year.

As long as I work on mourning my grief openly and
authentically, this year will be one of momentum and
positive personal growth and healing.

When I'm in grief, active mourning is the
linchpin resolution. It makes all other goals and
hopes possible. And conversely, a lack of active
mourning blocks healing and growth.

•

REFLECTION

When I'm in grief, I will commit myself to mourn.

Grief is my teacher

My grief is teaching me so much. It's teaching me what's most important to me. It's teaching me what I can jettison from my life because it no longer serves me. It's teaching me how much and in what ways I need other people.

I'm sometimes surprised at all the things I'm learning from my grief. And I'm sometimes regretful that I didn't learn these things earlier.

Even though it's hard to learn from loss, I'm being a mindful student. Because I know that if I integrate what I'm learning into my continuing life, I will live and love with meaning and purpose.

·

REFLECTION

My grief has awakened me.

I practice self-compassion

I've been torn apart by my grief. I am wounded.
I need and deserve tender, loving care.

When I'm kind to and patient with myself, I am
practicing tender, loving self-care.

When I catch myself being impatient with or
hard on myself, I stop, take a deep breath, and
remember to practice self-compassion.

·

REFLECTION

In living without judgment, I naturally feel
compassion for everyone, including myself.

Certain objects help me feel close to the person who died

Linking objects are items that belonged to the person who died, or remind me of them. Certain objects such as pieces of clothing or special belongings help me feel physically connected to the person I miss so much.

It's normal to hold onto and even cherish linking objects. Conversely, if I move to get rid of the personal belongings of the person who died too quickly, I might be avoiding my grief.

Objects that help me acknowledge and embrace my grief are helpful to have around.

●

REFLECTION

I recognize that my love is intangible and will always live inside me.

I'm working to make my life good again

The word "reconcile" comes from the
Middle English for "to make good again."
This is the essence of reconciliation in grief,
actually—to make my life good again.

Today, tomorrow, and every day,
I'm doing the work that it takes.

I have hope that my life will be good again.

I have faith that my life will be good again.

·

REFLECTION

As I allow myself to mourn, I'm on a path
to make my life good again.

I can say stop

When I catch myself in a grief behavior that doesn't serve me well, I can just say, "Stop!"

For example, if I become aware that I'm feeling ashamed of my grief or reticent to express it aloud, I can call myself out. "Stop it!" I can say. Or if someone else is judging or belittling my grief, I can kindly ask them to stop.

There's power in simply saying stop. When I create such a pause, I've created a space for a different, healthier behavior to begin.

●

REFLECTION
Awareness is the key to positive change.

My grief is just part of my life right now

I have many commitments and things going on in my present life. While I sometimes wish I could, I can't pause everything else in order to exclusively grieve and mourn.

Yet too much additional stress in my life can make my grief journey overwhelming. So I'm open to offloading extra commitments for the time being.

What steps can I take to destress my life right now? I'm looking into that.

·

REFLECTION

My default setting is to choose meaning, presence, and simplicity in my life.

I'm working on stepping outside of blame

In grief, blame—like anger—is often a protective mechanism. We sometimes blame other people, the person who died, or even ourselves. We might feel vindictive or justified in our blame.

Regardless of the circumstances surrounding the loss and whether anyone is actually "to blame," I'm learning that blame is part of our culture of grief avoidance. We're not good at acknowledging and embracing the pain of loss, death, and grief, so we often take a stance that erects a barrier between us and that normal and necessary pain.

That barrier is sometimes blame.

•

REFLECTION

When I feel blame of any kind, I step outside it and regard it with awareness and empathy.

It's OK to feel ambivalent

Our hearts can be both broken and mending
in the same moment.

The word "ambivalence" means to feel two
opposing ways at the same time. If I'm feeling
ambivalent, my heart might be both
grief-stricken and glad.

Ambivalence in grief is normal. I can feel
many things at once.

•

REFLECTION

I don't think in terms of this or that. I think in
terms of allowing whatever is.

I use goalsetting to help me foster hope and healing

I'm not overcommitting. I'm offloading any activities that are optional and that don't support my healing right now. I'm being patient with myself and freeing myself from too many expectations.

Yet at the same time, I know that I can use reasonable, limited goalsetting as a way of nurturing health and hope. Short-term goals might help me complete mourning activities. Longer-term goals might help me understand that my life still has meaning and purpose. Just-for-fun goals give me something to look forward to.

·

REFLECTION

I naturally move toward my heart-centered hopes and dreams.

I must say hello before I can say goodbye

While I've already said goodbye to the physical presence of my loved one, I'm struggling with figuring out how to say goodbye to our former relationship and the many ways their life intersected with mine.

I'm learning that before I can say goodbye to our relationship, I must first say hello to all of the ways that my life is now different. Hello, loss. Hello, grief. Hello, empty chair at the table. Hello, changing me.

As I move toward reconciliation, I will be saying more goodbyes. Goodbye, old routine. Goodbye, companionship. Goodbye, ever-present pain.

·

REFLECTION
I'm getting better at allowing—or saying hello to—
new realities as they arise.

My grief is a wilderness

My grief is a vast, mountainous, inhospitable forest. I'm in the wilderness now. I am in the midst of unfamiliar and often brutal surroundings. I'm cold and tired.

In the wilderness of my grief, I watch for healing touchstones. They are the signs that let me know I'm on the right path. Just as we cannot completely control nature, I can't completely master the wilderness of my grief. But I can become a master journeyer.

By following the touchstones, I will find my way out of the wilderness of my grief, and I will learn to make the most of my precious life.

•

REFLECTION

I will eventually leave the wilderness and find my way to gentler terrain.

My life constantly changes in ways I can't control

Our culture tells us an imaginary story about human life. It says that we grow, go to school, get a good job, get married, and have children. We work hard and succeed. We enjoy our friends, family, and eventually our children's children. We die happy, after a long, fulfilling life.

It's a fairytale. For one, our unique spirits may find meaning in different life trajectories. And for another, things happen all the time that preclude or take away our wishes and attachments. Change happens. Loss happens.

I'm learning that reconciling my grief has a lot to do with reconciling myself to the realities of unwanted change in life. Only in living with authenticity, presence, and love each day can I create a new story that tells the truth and honors the realities—and wonders—of life as it actually is.

·

REFLECTION

I ride atop the waves of change.

I understand that grief and mourning aren't the same thing

Grief is everything I think and feel inside of me about the loss.

Mourning is expressing those thoughts and feelings outside of myself.

Grief happens automatically after a loss. Mourning takes time and effort. Mourning is the work of grief, and mourning is how I heal.

•

REFLECTION

Putting my grief into action through mourning allows me to experience change and movement.

I'm not a body with a soul, I'm a soul with a body

When I can maintain awareness that
I'm fundamentally a soul inhabiting a body,
it becomes a little easier for me to see
my life and my loss as fleeting.

I'm only here on earth for a short while. Perhaps
I came from somewhere before I had a body, and
perhaps I will return there after my body is spent.

Practices that nurture my spirit help me maintain
this perspective. I think I'll spend at least fifteen
minutes on one of these activities today.

·

REFLECTION

I'm centered in my soul.

I've lost a witness

The person who died may have been one of
the few people who knew me really well.
We were close. Throughout our time together,
I saw them, and they saw me.

But now, they're no longer here to be their unique self
or to provide me with companionship. And they're
not here to see me! They knew me so well that I could
count on them to understand what I knew, thought,
and felt. They knew what I liked. They knew what I
disliked. They knew what I wore and looked like and
sounded like. They knew so much about me.

I'm grieving the loss of this special witness to my life.

.

REFLECTION

I understand the importance of being witnessed in life
and grief, so I seek to bear witness to others.

It's OK to ask, "Why me?"

Life isn't fair. While everyone suffers loss, some people seem to be dealt worse cards than others.

So if I feel I've gotten the short end of the stick in some way, it's OK for me to ask, "Why me?" Any feelings of injustice I might have are a normal part of my grief and my search for meaning.

Grievers will sometimes acknowledge that even though they've suffered a terrible loss, there are others who have it worse than them. This is always true, but it doesn't take away my need to grieve and mourn my unique loss.

•

REFLECTION

Asking "why me?" is often a normal and natural part of the unfolding of my grief.

My rituals comfort me

I can use daily rituals to comfort myself.

They might be as simple as having a cup of tea, taking a walk, or listening to music. Others might be more elaborate. Attending a worship service is also a ritual and so is meditating at the same time and in the same place each day.

Rituals can be faith-based or not, but all rituals are spiritual routines that free me from meaningless thought and soothe my soul. In helping me inhabit the present moment, rituals bring me closer to peace, healing, and the divine.

·

REFLECTION

Rituals invite my soul forward.

There are no rewards for speed

Grief work is hard work. Grief work is slow. My grief journey will take as long as it takes.

Whenever I feel impatient with my grief, I'll remember that there are no rewards for speed. I'll remember that resisting the natural pace of my grief will only make it harden. Instead, if I lean into and befriend my grief whenever I feel it—and especially if I take the time to express it outside of myself in some way—I'll notice that it softens. I'm learning to trust that my pain will ease over time.

·

REFLECTION

Giving attention to my grief creates the natural movement I desire.

I don't know what will happen tomorrow

Most of us go through life expecting that tomorrow will be a lot like today. For long stretches of time, we can be lulled into complacency. We assume that our weeks and months will unfold in routine ways.

But tomorrow is promised to none of us. The death of my loved one has made me acutely aware of this reality. And now I realize that I don't actually know what will happen tomorrow.

How I respond to the reality of life's uncertainty is up to me. I may naturally feel anxious about it, worried about what will happen next. But I'm becoming aware that I can choose to surrender to the uncertainty instead, and simply live in gratitude for this day.

•

REFLECTION

Life is one surprise after another, but the deepest me remains steadfast.

I can make a vision board

When I'm in need of some inspiration and hope on my grief journey, I can make a vision board.

Using pages torn from old magazines, or photos and artwork I print from the internet, I can gather up images and sayings that capture my hopes and dreams. Then I can arrange and glue or tack them on a piece of cardboard, poster board, or bulletin board.

My vision board can become a touchstone for my healing. When I'm feeling stuck in my grief, my vision board will remind me that I do want to live an ongoing life of meaning, connection, and joy. I can also use my vision board as part of a daily affirmation practice.

·

REFLECTION

I visualize a peaceful, meaningful future for myself.

I can do one small thing

Some days the best I can do is survive.
Sometimes my loss feels so overwhelming and my
pain so great that all I can do is seek comfort and
take care of myself the best I can.

But other days, maybe like today, I have a
little more traction on the path of my grief.
I have a little more energy and momentum.
On those days, I can set my intention to do one
small thing to actively mourn and integrate
my loss just a tiny bit more.

Today I will do one small thing.

·

REFLECTION
I naturally allow, embrace, and integrate.

I need to feel it to heal it

Whatever feelings arise when I'm grieving are
authentic, necessary feelings. They are my truth
for the moment. They all belong.

My job is to acknowledge each feeling, sit with it,
name it, and express it.

Befriending my feelings in this way helps
me understand them as well as the thoughts
that create them. Only through allowing
myself to feel can I heal.

·

REFLECTION

I'm kind to every feeling I have because I know
that everything belongs.

I'm open to seeing a grief counselor

Mental healthcare is just as important as physical healthcare. If I'm struggling with my grief, I'll find a compassionate grief counselor, either online or in my community.

Seeing a grief counselor doesn't mean there's anything wrong with me. It just means that I might benefit from talking to a compassionate, objective listener and a professional who can walk beside me for a while on my grief journey.

Seeing a grief counselor is simply good self-care. I'm proud of myself for taking good care of me.

•

REFLECTION

Mental health professionals are part of my care team, just like physical health professionals are.

I'm finding the biggest joys in the smallest moments

As I emerged from the fog of early grief, life seemed different. Part of the difference was my loss and my pain, but another part was that my surroundings and some of the sights, sounds, smells, textures, and tastes I encountered during my activities of daily living seemed strangely new.

I began to notice things in a new way. Not all of the differences felt pleasant or remarkable, but some did. Just the capacity to be more aware of the small things gave me a new appreciation for life.

I'm learning that life's biggest joys are to be found in the smallest moments, if only I pay attention and nurture gratitude.

·

REFLECTION
When I'm aware, I can find joy in any moment.

My explosive emotions are forms of protest

Anger, hate, blame, terror, resentment, rage, and jealousy are normal feelings in grief. They're the explosive emotions, and they are forms of protest.

I didn't want the person I love to die, so I'm objecting. I may direct my anger and other explosive emotions at any number of people: a family member, a friend, someone who had something to do with my loved one's care, the person who died, or myself.

As long as my anger doesn't harm me or others (including emotionally), I have every right to feel and express it. I'm working on finding constructive ways to express my anger.

·

REFLECTION
I know that anger masks fear and sorrow.
When I feel angry, I dig deeper to become aware
of the feelings beneath the anger.

I count my blessings

I'm blessed. My life has purpose and meaning,
even without the presence of the person who died.

If I'm hurting and having a hard time feeling
the blessings in my life for a while, that's OK.
The hurt comes first.

But even if I feel unlucky, even if I worry that
I'm destined to be unhappy, even if it feels
like the universe is conspiring against me,
I also know deep down that I still have much
to be thankful for. When I'm ready,
I'll work on counting my blessings.

•

REFLECTION

Life is a blessing. And since life includes
both wonderful and awful experiences,
I'm blessed to be here for all of it.

What if this were my last time…?

I know that finding and expressing my gratitude is a practice that helps me live for today and balance my natural grief with the need to go on. But sometimes it's hard to feel grateful, especially when I'm hurting due to my loss—and possibly other things in my life aren't going well either.

I can try to initiate my gratitude by asking myself, "What if this were my last time _____?" For example, if I have to rake leaves and I'm feeling irritated or sad, I can ask myself, "What if this were my last time raking leaves? What if something were to happen to me and I could no longer do this? Or what if I were to die before next year's leaf-raking time came around?"

Intentionally cultivating a little mortality awareness can help me live this day with more presence and gratitude.

·

REFLECTION
As much as possible, I live every experience like it might be my last.

I make time each day for spirituality

My spirituality is so intertwined with my grief
and healing that making time for it every day
is one of my very top priorities.

Just fifteen minutes or half an hour each day
dedicated to a spiritual practice of my choosing can
completely transform my outlook and my capacity to
effectively mourn my grief.

If I haven't yet settled on spiritual practices that
work for me, that's OK. I'll keep trying new ones.
Meditation, prayer, yoga, engaging with nature,
attending religious or spiritual services, and many
more simple, soulful practices are available to buoy
my spirit right here and now.

·

REFLECTION
Because my spirit is my essence,
my spirituality is essential.

I'm careful with love

My grief has made me more aware of actively and generously loving the people who are still present in my life.

When I care about someone, I tell them so, and I treat them lovingly. I'm also very careful not to express myself unkindly, because words matter and have lasting effects

The poet Kahlil Gibran wisely wrote, "Between what is said and not meant, and what is meant and not said, most of love is lost." I no longer want to be someone who loses any tiny, precious drops of love.

•

REFLECTION

Love is truth. Hate and other unkind feelings are ego.

I think I can

Like the Little Engine That Could, I think I can.

Since my loss, I may have had to take on new roles and responsibilities. This can be uncomfortable and scary, but I've realized that I can actually do more than I gave myself credit for.

As I encounter my changed life and new challenges, and opportunities present themselves, I'm trying to think, "OK, I'll try that" instead of, "Nope, I can't do that."

Not only is this mindset helping me navigate my grief, it's showing me that I can pleasantly surprise myself sometimes.

·

REFLECTION
I know I can.

I open my heart wide

Because I loved someone deeply, I'm now grieving deeply. That's the bargain of human life.

Right after the loss, at first I needed to withdraw and close up my heart for a while. I needed to protect the wound from any further pain. But now I'm opening my heart back up again. I'm mourning openly and authentically, letting my grief feelings out, and I'm allowing new feelings and experiences in.

When I open my heart wide, I truly live.

•

REFLECTION
There's nothing more beautiful than a wide-open heart.

I'm under reconstruction

My loss tore me apart, and now
I'm under reconstruction.

This reconstruction process is time-consuming
and messy. Like any major overhaul, it gets worse
before it gets better. It's wearing and noisy.
And it's not orderly, either. I don't even know what
I'm going to be like when the project is finished.

But nonetheless, every day I put on
my hardhat, and I get to work.

•

REFLECTION
I engage with all things creative and constructive.

I'm listening for grief tapes— and turning them off

I've been around long enough to have absorbed all kinds of beliefs about grief and mourning. They're like tapes that play in my brain—consciously and subconsciously—all the time.

In our grief-avoidant culture, these tapes are usually wrongheaded. So I'm trying to notice the tapes I'm listening to, examine them one at a time, and discard those that are harming me instead of helping me.

When I hear the tape that says, "You just need to get over this," for instance, I toss it out. Ditto the tapes that say, "You're doing this wrong" and "Your life is over." And there are many more. I have a feeling I'm going to be getting rid of a lot of old tapes.

●

REFLECTION

I attempt to see misconceptions for what they are.

The only special occasion is now

My loss is teaching me the importance
of living in the moment.

After all, all I ever had with the person who died
were moments. Most of them weren't memorable
occasions. Instead, they were inconsequential,
everyday hours and days of coexisting.
But oh how I yearn to have those moments back,
so I could notice and celebrate them as they
deserve to have been noticed and celebrated.

The only special occasion is this moment.
I'm working on doing a better job of
treating it that way.

·

REFLECTION
Life is a special occasion.

I accept myself just as I am

I know I'm not perfect, but sometimes my
grief has me thinking that I'm *really* a mess.
When my thoughts and feelings are chaotic, when
I can't seem to get anything accomplished, or
when I do or say something I regret,
I feel ashamed of myself.

What's wrong with me?

The truth is that there's nothing wrong with me!
I'm just grieving, and grief is messy. If my grief
circumstances are extra complicated, I might need
some help from a counselor or support group—
but even if that's the case, there's nothing wrong
with me. So I accept myself just as I am.

·

REFLECTION
In the moment, I accept everything just as it is.

When I love myself well, I become more lovable

Self-care in grief is so important. I'm wounded, and I need to take excellent care of myself so that I have the energy and fortitude it takes to do the hard work of mourning and to heal.

Part of my self-care regimen involves bolstering my self-esteem, especially if I've been feeling inadequate. Taking intentional care of myself physically, cognitively, emotionally, socially, and spiritually builds my sense of self-worth.

When I love myself well, my life becomes richer and more fulfilling. I appreciate solitude more, and when I'm in the company of others, I'm a more whole, engaged, giving person. Loving myself well helps me feel better and also leads to stronger connections and relationships with others.

•

REFLECTION
I treat everyone, including myself, kindly and lovingly.

Will I transcend my grief?

I sometimes wonder what my grief will feel like years from now. I know I will still love. I know I will still feel the loss and some degree of pain. But what else will I feel? Will I feel peace? Will I feel wiser? What will I have learned?

To transcend means "to go beyond the range or limits of." Even now I feel myself changing. I am different now than I was before, and I continue to evolve. I can look to the future and see that I will surely go beyond the range or limits of my current self.

Therefore I set my intention today to move toward a future me that lives as fully, deeply, and meaningfully as possible.

·

REFLECTION

I am spiritually without limits, and I intend to soar.

I can support someone else grieving this loss

When I'm ready to reemerge a little into the world, one thing I can do to engage with my own grief is to support someone else in theirs.

Offering my care and empathy to someone grieving the same loss as I am can be helpful to both of us. If I reach out, I'm helping the other person with the sixth need of mourning, but I'm also helping myself with the same need. We can talk together about the person who died. We can share our memories. Our grief isn't the same, and learning from each other about our unique thoughts and feelings can be a surprising catalyst for healing.

•

REFLECTION

Being of service to others gives my life meaning.

I recognize when I'm postponing my grief

Sometimes I put off my grief. I think of a memory, feel a twinge, or experience a griefburst…and immediately try to distract myself.

Of course, I can't always stop what I'm doing to embrace and express my grief. In those cases, it's normal and healthy to postpone a full encounter with my painful thoughts and feelings.

But when I put off my grief too often and too long, it can become unembarked grief. I must not deny its rightful and necessary presence in my life. A bit of denial now and then is healthy. Too much denial is extremely unhealthy.

·

REFLECTION
While part of me wants to put off my grief,
I realize I must experience it.

My body might sympathize with the death

When people care deeply about someone who dies, they sometimes develop new ways to identify with the loss and feel close to that person. One way is by relating to the physical symptoms associated with the person's illness or death.

If I experience physical symptoms like this, it's OK. I'll visit my primary care provider to ensure I'm healthy. And I will be patient and understanding with my body as it responds to the loss.

•

REFLECTION
As I listen to my body, I realize
I'm listening to my grief.

What am I giving up by worrying right now?

When my natural, intermittent grief fears get stuck in the ongoing groove of worry, I know it's time to work on self-care practices that help me live more mindfully.

Meditating, cultivating gratitude, and immersing myself in healthy activities in which I lose myself are three possibilities. Another is stopping to ask myself: What am I giving up by worrying right now?

In every moment, I have the choice to be stuck in my head or engaged in the reality of what surrounds me. When I'm stuck in my head worrying, I'm not mindfully present. So if I ask myself what I'm giving up by worrying right now, I'm forced to look around me and see what or who else I could be engaging with instead.

·

REFLECTION

I choose not to spend my precious time worrying.

I can take a retreat

I can't run away from my grief, because wherever I go, I carry it inside me. But I can take a retreat from my everyday life. I can go somewhere new and different, and the change of scenery will help me discover new ways of looking at things.

Retreats to quiet, natural environments can be especially restful and reinvigorating. While there I will still encounter my grief, but I can do it in a place that isn't taxing in other ways. The peace and beauty of nature center and calm me.

If I can't get away, I may still be able to take a retreat inside my own home. I can spend a day or a weekend in my bedroom resting and pampering myself.

·

REFLECTION

Allowing time for retreat provides me new perspectives.

When I'm feeling ignored or misunderstood, it's time to talk about it

Sometimes my grief is so constant and present inside me that I forget that other people can't necessarily see it or understand it. Because grief is invisible, I can feel overlooked or misunderstood.

When this happens, I need to express my grief. I need to mourn. I need to talk about it with compassionate, good listeners.

The people who care about me want to support me, but they can't read my mind and my heart. I need to tell them what I'm thinking and feeling.

•

REFLECTION
Being fully present to others creates more opportunity to express myself authentically and to bear witness to their authentic selves as well.

Happy Valentine's Day

Oh my dear, I'm missing you today.

You aren't here, but my love for you still is. I think I'll share something about that love with someone else today. I'll tell someone about you, I'll share your photo and a memory on social media, or I'll make your favorite meal for someone. I'll give someone your favorite flowers, or I'll bring them your favorite candy.

I'd give anything to have you back again. The next best thing is bringing your memory to life in some small way on this day that honors love.

·

REFLECTION
I celebrate love every day.

I mourn in doses

Grief is not a "hurry-up-and-get-this-over" kind of experience. It takes time—often years—to reconcile a significant loss.

And so on days when my grief is weighing me down, I remember that I can't do it all at once. It's healthier to find ways to balance my grief with my ongoing life.

When I feel my grief, I express it. But I do so in doses. I dedicate time to sharing my grief outside of myself, and then I turn my attention back to living. Back and forth, back and forth.

·

REFLECTION

I live in the moment, and in the moment I express myself in ways that help me live a rich, connected, purposeful life.

I'm a teacher of grief literacy

Through intentional study and engagement, I've been learning so much about grief and mourning. I've learned that they're normal and necessary. I've learned that my grief is simply part of my love and that I need to express it openly and honestly. I've learned that I have six needs of mourning, including receiving support from other people.

Our culture tends to avoid grief. It's grief illiterate. But I'm not grief illiterate now, so when I'm ready, I can help model for, mentor, and teach others.

Better grief literacy in this world will lead to better mental health in this world.

·

REFLECTION

My ways of being in the world help lift others.

What I resist, persists

In grief, it's so easy to get stuck in anger or
resistance. Those are normal feelings,
but they can also become traps.

If I feel myself getting stuck in resisting some
aspect of the loss or my grief—something I don't
like and wish I could change but can't—I'll take
a step back and shine my self-compassionate
awareness on it. I will see that in continuing to
resist some reality that I can't control, I'm only
increasing my own suffering.

I want my pain to soften, not persist.
So I'll work on letting go of resistance.

·

REFLECTION
I witness, accept, and allow what is.

My grief isn't predictable or orderly

People talk about the stages of grief, but my grief isn't shaped like that. For one, I experience a mixture of feelings at the same time. For two, I sometimes return to feelings I had earlier in my journey. And for three, I rarely know where my grief will take me next.

Each day, my grief is what it is. I don't have to concern myself with where I "should be" in my grief. Instead, I am where I am, and that is always enough.

·

REFLECTION
I embrace the chaos that is life.

I step outside my comfort zone

Grief is outside my comfort zone, I'll tell you that.
If anything's uncomfortable, it's grief.

So since I'm outside my comfort zone already,
I might as well try some new things.
What do I have to lose?

I can do something I've always wanted to.
Or I can say yes when a friend invites me to
expand my horizons.

I might find that some of the boundaries
of my old comfort zone were actually false
and were holding me back.

•

REFLECTION
I'm open to trying new things.

Regrets and "if-onlys" are normal

Regrets, if-onlys, and self-blame are common and natural feelings after the death of someone loved. If only I had said this… If only I had done that… If only I hadn't said or done that…

It's normal to think about how things could have been different. It's normal to think about how I could have acted differently. But that is the human condition. We are imperfect, and we don't always get second chances.

I'm learning to be compassionate with myself and forgive past mistakes. I am also learning to express my regrets out loud to others because, counterintuitively, it helps them fade away.

·

REFLECTION

I accept my imperfect past as essential to my imperfect present.

I act with awareness

The normal and necessary emotions of grief have tossed me about. But the more I befriend them, the more I see that they can flow through me without controlling me.

When I allow myself to feel my emotions with this awareness, I become more capable of acting with awareness. I realize I no longer have to respond impulsively.

I can choose to act consciously and intentionally. This in turn allows me to create the life I want.

·

REFLECTION
Conscious awareness of what I think
and feel allows me to befriend my grief.

I speak a love language

In his landmark 1995 book *The Five Love Languages*, author Dr. Gary Chapman introduced the idea that human beings feel cared for by others in five primary ways:

1. Receiving gifts
2. Spending quality time together
3. Hearing words of affirmation
4. Being the beneficiary of acts of service
5. Experiencing physical touch

Which is my preferred love language? I'm learning to be aware of it, and I'm learning to ask others to support me by "speaking" that language.

•

REFLECTION

I understand that my love language will be reflected in my grief language.

I'm putting off big decisions

Especially if I'm early in my grief journey, I'm likely in no fit state to be making major life changes. Sometimes mourners make rash decisions shortly after a death in an effort to obliterate the pain and "move forward," but they often end up regretting these choices.

So unless I have no choice but to make big life decisions right now, I'm putting them off for a couple of years. In the meantime, I'm using what energy I have to survive, embrace and express my grief, and consider what I really and truly want to do with the remainder of my precious days here on earth.

·

REFLECTION

I make major life decisions in alignment with meaning and purpose.

The love is still there

I still love the person who died. I will always love the person who died. The nature of our relationship has changed, and so I can no longer express and share that love in the ways I desperately wish I could. But even so, I feel the love.

Over time and through active mourning, the pain will begin to soften. Is it already softening a little? But the love—that will only deepen and grow burnished in memory.

Grief is my love right now. They are two sides of the same precious coin. Eventually the coin will, more and more often, land love side up.

·

REFLECTION

This book is encouraging me to express my grief. On any given day, I can also choose to express my ongoing, here-and-now love.

My past experiences with death and loss shape my current grief

I didn't arrive at this current loss an unmarked page. I have experienced other losses in my life, and those losses have given me expectations, hopes, and fears about this grief journey.

Yet I'm also learning that I can choose to be a spiritual optimist in grief. If past losses ended up creating unreconciled pain and pessimism in me about loss and grief, I can revisit those prior losses and work through any carried pain.

Shakespeare said what's past is prologue. This is true, but I can also choose a new plot twist in the present.

•

REFLECTION

I step into each new moment without expectation or prejudice.

Remembering is also re-membering

In the physical plane, my relationship with the person who died has ended. But on the emotional and spiritual planes, my relationship with the person who died continues. First, I still love this precious person. And second, I will always have a relationship of memory with them.

I can talk about or write out favorite memories. I can hold special keepsakes that link me to the person who died. I can display and look through photos. I can visit places of special significance that stimulate memories of times spent together.

Remembering helps me re-member—put back together something that has been torn apart.

·

REFLECTION

I remember with gratitude.

I won't always feel how I feel today

However I feel today, I know that it's temporary. I'm learning that my thoughts and feelings change from day to day, week to week, and year to year.

I am also learning that the more I embrace my painful feelings and express them outside of myself (mourn), the less powerful they become.

If I actively mourn, over time my grief will soften.

•

REFLECTION

My feelings may be fickle, but underneath them is a still, quiet, eternal love.

I turn toward kindness, compassion, and love

In early grief, people often need to withdraw and self-isolate. This is a survival instinct, to shut down for a period of days or weeks and crawl into the cocoon of grief shock.

But after a while, when it's time to reemerge, it can be hard knowing how to navigate each day. What should I be doing from hour to hour?

I'm learning that if I choose to turn toward kindness, compassion, and love, my days are a little more tolerable. Like a flower turns toward the sun, I can open myself to the people who are trying to companion me in my grief—in whatever ways they are capable of.

·

REFLECTION

I glow with kindness, compassion, and love.

I move toward my grief

Sometimes people imply that feeling bad is a choice. They tell me that I deserve to be happy, and they congratulate me if I talk about "more positive" things. They encourage me to move away from my grief instead of toward it.

But when I'm feeling my grief, I need to move toward it. I need to turn toward it, acknowledge it, and express it. I need to feel it to heal it. Denial and distraction are OK sometimes, but if I deny and distract too much, I'm only setting myself up for long-term problems.

·

REFLECTION
I seek out opportunities to be vulnerable and authentic because that is where the magic happens.

My physical wellbeing is interconnected with my emotional and spiritual wellbeing

My grief journey affects me physically, cognitively, emotionally, socially, and spiritually. Physical symptoms of grief are normal, but if I'm unwell physically, it's hard for me to work on the other aspects of my grief.

I take care of myself physically, and when I am feeling unwell, I visit my primary care providers and work to enhance my health.

⦿

REFLECTION

Caring for my body is among my most important priorities.

Judging and loving are like oil and water

After a loss, it's tempting to judge. Like anger, judgment feels active and better than sadness, which is passive and often goes hand-in-hand with feelings of helplessness.

So during my grief journey, I might have found myself judging. I might judge other family members or friends over their response to the loss. Feeling inadequate or badly behaved, I might judge myself. I might even judge the person who died because they made mistakes.

But judgment blocks love. The two things can't really coexist. So if I instead surrender to the imperfections and mysteries of humanity, I forgive all shortcomings and extend empathy in lieu of judgment. I love others, and I love myself. Love feels so much better, and it also gives momentum to my healing.

•

REFLECTION
I usher out judgment and invite love in.

I'm allowed to be myself in grief

People tell me I should be doing this and not
that as I grieve. Sometimes they're right.
Sometimes they give me good advice—
advice that's in keeping with philosophies
I like and books I'm reading.

But even when I agree in principle with good
grief and mourning advice, I can't always follow
all of it. Either I'm not ready, or parts of it
just aren't me (or both).

I'm allowed to be myself as I grieve and mourn.
I don't have to be a perfect, superhero griever to move
toward healing and reconcile my grief.
I'm doing the very best I know to do.

·

REFLECTION
I am being myself.

I make it a priority to get good sleep

Loss often disturbs sleep. I might be experiencing insomnia, or I might be sleeping too much yet still not feel rested.

If I'm having sleep issues, I don't let them slide. Instead, I work to ensure my sleep habits are as healthy and effective as possible. And if I'm still having trouble sleeping, I see my primary care provider and maybe even a sleep specialist.

Good sleep is the foundation of wellness. I can't mourn effectively and move toward healing if I'm not getting good sleep.

·

REFLECTION

Grief naturally disturbs my sleep, so I must allow myself to rest and renew whenever possible.

We all need companionship in grief

One of the six needs of mourning is to
let others help me—now and always.
As I'm moving through my grief, I'm learning
that I need others *and* they need me.

Just as we all need companionship during
"the good times" in life, we all need
companionship in grief. And when
I really look around at my friends, colleagues,
neighbors, and loved ones, I become aware that
many of them are grieving, too.

Grief is pervasive. We need each other.
Companionship and camaraderie are
always essential.

·

REFLECTION

I'm an integral part of the lives of many others,
and they're an integral part of mine.

I am allowing myself to change

My loss tore me apart. It shattered me into a million pieces.

As I actively mourn, I'm finding ways to pick up the pieces and put them back together. But the reassembled version of me isn't the exact same me I was before. I'm finding that I have new attitudes, new likes and dislikes, new habits and tendencies, new priorities.

I'm changing, and so I'm not fighting these changes. These changes are normal and necessary.

•

REFLECTION
The outer circumstances of my life and the outer "me" are constantly in flux.
Grief creates a natural transformation.

The possibilities are endless

My grief is a transitional experience.
Change is hard, and this movement from
"before" to "after" is painful.

But even in the midst of my pain, I'm starting
to feel some doors opening. I'm realizing
that many of my old assumptions about
my life are no longer valid.

Within reason, I can do anything I want. I can be
anything I want to be. I can open myself to life in
infinite ways. This gaping tear in my heart is the
place where new possibilities are entering.

·

REFLECTION
I can.

If today is a bad day, that's OK

Some days are just plain terrible, no matter how mindfully present and allowing I am.

But a bad day is just that—one bad day. I can still go to bed that night with trust and hope in my heart that the next day will be better. And on that next day, I can use the power of intention to make it better by taking fantastic, self-compassionate care of myself, by focusing on activities and people that give my life meaning and purpose, and by devoting time to my spirituality.

Bad days happen, and that's OK.

·

REFLECTION

The more mindful I become, the more I realize that many happenings I've thought of as "bad" actually don't matter at all.

I can and will heal

To heal in grief is to become whole again,
to integrate my grief into myself and to
learn to continue my changed life with
fullness and meaning.

In grief, healing is not curing. I will always grieve.
My grief will always be a part of me. But through
befriending my grief and active mourning, it will
become a fully integrated part of who I am, just
like all significant experiences in my life.

My grief will no longer dominate my days and
monopolize my nights. Instead, it will become
more of a bittersweet constant in the
background of my continuing life.

·

REFLECTION

I'm not only healing, I'm being
transformed by my grief.

I give myself permission to fail sometimes

The more I learn about the basic principles of grief and mourning, the more I understand what I could and should be doing with my grief. But I'm not always great about applying this understanding.

It's like diet and exercise. I know what I'm supposed to do to be healthy, but I don't always do it.

So I'm giving myself permission to fail now and then. Let's say I go through periods of ignoring my grief or judging myself harshly. I know that both of these are unhealthy in grief, but sometimes I just get stuck in unhealthy behaviors. Life is challenging, and I'm not perfect.

•

REFLECTION
It's not failure. It's learning.

If I'm in the early months
of my grief journey, I am coming
to understand that my grief
will probably hurt more
before it hurts less

New grief comes with a natural anesthetic. Immediately after the person I love died, I found myself numbed by shock and disbelief.

As the newness began to wear off, the anesthetic began to wear off too. I started to feel the ache of my grief more sharply.

But I'm also finding that when I befriend my pain, it softens. In fact, acknowledging and befriending the natural pain of grief is a balm that truly heals instead of numbing temporarily.

•

REFLECTION
The initial shock helped me survive, but now
the grief comes in waves.

I nurture my curiosity

When I'm curious about things, life is more interesting. Whenever I feel that impulse to see, learn, visit, or explore something, I know that I'm continuing to engage with actively living my one wild and precious life. I'm feeling and acting on my life force.

To keep that spark alive, I intentionally nurture it. When possible and when I have the energy, I go out of my way to give myself simple opportunities to see new things, meet new people, learn new information, and try new activities.

They say variety is the spice of life. I honor that.

·

REFLECTION

The world is my playground.

My grief might make me wonder if life is worth it

Sometimes people experiencing the pain of grief wonder if life is worth it. "It would be so much easier to not be here," they might think.

It's normal to want to not hurt. It's normal to feel the pain is too much to bear.

There's a difference between these normal thoughts and suicidal planning, though. If passing thoughts turn into suicidal plans or structure, that means it's time for me to get help right away.

Sometimes tunnel vision prevents people from seeing choices. I have the choice to befriend and mourn my grief, with the support of others, and find my way back to hope and meaning again.

·

REFLECTION

If I find myself questioning my desire to live, I reach out for the support I need and deserve.

I'm becoming more patient

Grief is slow. Even though I'm actively mourning, it's taking a long time for my painful thoughts and feelings to soften.

So I'm learning to be patient—with myself and with others. There's no use being impatient. That only increases my suffering and damages my relationships.

Patience, in life and in grief, is hard-won wisdom in action.

•

REFLECTION
Everything takes as long as it takes, and that's OK.

If I feel guilty in any way, I need to talk about it

After the death of someone loved, many grievers feel guilty about something.

Some feel guilty about past events or behaviors. Some feel guilty that they are still alive while the person they love is not. Some feel guilty because they have a sense of release or relief after a death. Some feel guilty when they allow themselves to experience happiness or joy during their time of grief.

These and other circumstances may give rise to guilt. If this happens to me, it doesn't mean I've done anything wrong. It simply means that I'm having normal, conflicting, human feelings and need to talk them out.

•

REFLECTION
Guilt is usually a story I tell myself.
It is not my truth or essence.

My supporters come and go

As a culture, we're not good at grief support. We're not good at grief *honesty*. Even though it's an everyday part of life, we don't talk often or authentically enough about death and grief.

So…compassionate listeners and companions can be hard to come by. And even when I do find someone kind to share my grief with, they may not be available to me months from now.

My cast of supporters changes from season to season and year to year. This revolving door can feel hurtful sometimes, but it's normal. Maintaining empathy over time is difficult, and people are constantly facing their own challenges and losses. But still, I reach out, and I try to connect.

·

REFLECTION
When I'm with someone else,
I am present and kind to them.

I'm filling the gaps

When my loved one died, they left gaps in my life. The roles they played in my world and the times of companionship and connection we shared are now empty.

The holes they left behind are so painful to encounter and mourn.

Yet as I actively work on the six needs of mourning over time, I'm finding that the gaps are becoming less pronounced. Nothing and no one can ever replace the person who died, but the mosaic of my life is jostling around, and different people and activities are settling into some of the nooks and crannies.

•

REFLECTION
While I'll always have my holes, I can still have meaning and purpose in my life.

I move toward the light of healing

The light of healing in grief is not exactly a light at the end of the tunnel. It's not a fixed end point or perfect state of bliss. Bittersweet is as sweet as it gets.

Everything in life is comprised of both darkness and light. Life is made up of people, places, actions, things, and experiences that are mixtures of both. Healing is like this, too.

I can think of the light of healing as the thoughts and feelings I want to experience more of. Hope. Gratitude. Happiness. Joy. Love. Peace. The more I make friends with the darkness, the more my capacity for these light-filled thoughts and feelings grows.

·

REFLECTION
There is a lightness that comes from living
from a place of equanimity and hope.

My grief is my friend

My grief is my love in a different form. It's painful, yes, but it is a pain I am experiencing because I have been fortunate enough to love.

Just as love has been my friend, so too is grief my friend.

When I'm feeling my grief, I will welcome it like a friend. I will sit with it and listen to it. I will honor it, and I will learn from it. The more I befriend my grief and learn to understand it as part of my love, the better I will be able to integrate it into my ongoing life.

●

REFLECTION

I'm grateful to have loved, and so I'm grateful for my grief.

My loved one left behind a legacy

The person who died is no longer here with me—but their legacy is. Their ordinary life touched people and had an impact.

People who live seemingly unremarkable lives still leave behind a legacy after they die. I have the opportunity to recognize my loved one's legacy and help carry it forward on their behalf. For example, I can support a cause my loved one was passionate about. Or I can carry on a family ritual they were a part of. Or I can give gifts that they would have given, tend gardens that they would have tended (real gardens and metaphorical ones), and nurture relationships that were important to them.

I'm finding meaning in carrying on their legacy.

•

REFLECTION

Carrying on my loved one's legacy is part of my legacy.

If I find myself stuck in my grief, that means I need a bit of help

I might get stuck on some particular thought or feeling in my grief. I might feel like I just can't get past it.

Some mourners get stuck in anger about something related to a loss. Some get stuck in guilt. Others get stuck in anxiety or depression.

If I'm at an impasse in my grief, that just means I need some help getting past it. Seeing a compassionate grief counselor for a while is a good way to get unstuck and regain momentum.

·

REFLECTION

When I'm feeling stuck, I can commit myself to getting unstuck.

Death isn't a punishment

My mind might try to tell me stories about what happened in order to create a narrative that makes sense. It might say I deserve this loss for some reason. Or maybe it will say that the person who died deserved it.

But death isn't a punishment. It's a normal part of human life. Everyone dies at some point and in some way. Not everyone dies a peaceful death at the age of ninety. In fact, lots of people die young or in middle age, for all kinds of reasons.

If I can learn to see death objectively, as a normal, no-one-escapes-it outcome, I can put down the dirty pain of my mind's punishment story and just mourn the clean pain that comes after someone I love is no longer here.

.

REFLECTION
Life comes and goes, and its timing is often a mystery.

Meaning can come from lots of places

As I search to find meaning after the death of someone loved, I realize it can be found in lots of ways and places.

There is meaning in the life of the precious person who lived and died. I can look for ways to carry that meaning forward.

And for me, apart from the person who died, within my own singular life, there is also meaning. I'm building a new self-identity, and along the way I'm (re)discovering what gives me a sense of meaning and purpose. I'm on the hunt for people, places, ideas, and actions that light my divine spark and give me not just ho-hum reasons but wonderful reasons to get out of bed in the morning.

•

REFLECTION

Every life moment inherently contains meaning, if I only notice it.

My grief won't overpower me

I've been afraid of my grief. There have been times when I've avoided, suppressed, or denied it because I was fearful that it would overpower me and I wouldn't survive.

But as I've learned to befriend my grief, slowly and over time, I've realized it's nothing to be afraid of. It's simply my love in a different form.

My grief is painful and challenging, yes, but it's not a fearsome enemy. Even when it rages and howls, I now understand that deep down, it's a tender, vulnerable part of me that simply needs my love and attention.

•

REFLECTION

My true self can never be overpowered, come what may.

I'm creative

Being creative simply means acting on the impulse to make something that wasn't there before. Lots of people say they're not creative because they haven't learned how to paint pictures or write stories or make crafts.

Yet, everyone is creative. When I make a meal with care, I'm being creative. When I venture out on a new hiking trail, I'm being creative. When I dig a garden, I'm being creative.

I'm a naturally creative person because I bring new things into this world. All humans are. If I think of myself as uncreative, I'm doing myself a disservice, especially during my grief journey. Exploring my innate creativity helps me create a new self-identity, search for meaning, and foster hope.

•

REFLECTION

I can allow myself to be creative.

I see opportunities, not obstacles

On my journey through the wilderness of grief, I sometimes get stuck. I sometimes encounter obstacles that I have a hard time passing through.

And sometimes in my life, challenging circumstances arise that are obstacles to my security and wellbeing.

But even though there are real obstacles, and I need to take the time to grieve and mourn difficult realities, I know that those same obstacles are also opportunities. "What can I learn from this?" I ask. "How can I be present to my life despite this? How can I embrace changes that I can't control? What new meaning and purpose might arise as a result of this?"

·

REFLECTION

Every day is an opportunity. Every day is a gift.

My relationships are changing

Some of my relationships with friends and family members have shifted since the death. I'm learning that not everyone knows how to be supportive to a loved one who is grieving. I'm also finding that certain people are naturally good at it.

If I feel hurt or angry about any perceived lack of support, I share my feelings. But I try to refrain from blaming and accusations. I use "I statements" to express how I feel.

Over time, relationships change. That is the nature of human life.

·

REFLECTION

I understand that how people behave is a reflection of their own life journeys, not of me.

I'm appreciating my transformation

My journey through grief is changing me. The more I move through the wilderness of my grief, actively mourning along the way, the more I realize that I'm not the same person I was before.

It's not just that some of the outer circumstances of my life have changed. It's that I'm changing in fundamental ways at the core of my being.

I'm changing and growing. And when I notice that I'm changing in positive ways, I stop to acknowledge and appreciate my transformation.

·

REFLECTION

I am not so much changing as revealing my essence, which was there all along.

I can think beyond my present reality

At times during my grief journey, my present reality may be really, really tough. All kinds of difficult circumstances can converge, and I might find myself in despair.

If this happens, I can reach out for lifelines, including the support of others, spiritual mentorship, professional counseling, and more. But I can also work to recognize that my present reality is temporary.

Visualizing the future I desire is one tool. Remembering that I've been in difficult circumstances before but have gotten through them is another. Fostering hope by grabbing hold of any people and activities that help me know there is good to come is another.

·

REFLECTION

I live in the present. If the present is really hard, I live in this one moment, second by second.

I spend quality time with others

While one meaningful relationship in my life has come to an end, and I must now grieve and mourn that loss, I can also focus on other meaningful relationships in my life.

My close friends, family members, and loved ones help me with my grief. Spending quality time with them as often as I want to will not only help me heal, it will also strengthen the bonds of connection that make life worth living again.

Nurturing meaningful relationships takes an investment of time and energy, but it's without a doubt one of the best ways there is to spend time and energy.

·

REFLECTION

I am committed to being kind and present to the people in my life.

I love to laugh

My grief contains lots of pain, yes, but it's also big enough to contain happiness and laughter.

I can remember humorous memories. I can watch funny movies and comedians. I can take part in activities that are enjoyable. I can spend time with people who love life and who make me laugh.

Laughter stimulates chemicals in my brain that suppress stress hormones. Laughter also helps my breathing and circulation. I try to build at least a little laughter into each day.

•

REFLECTION
My natural impulse is to smile, feel gratitude, seek joy, and enjoy laughter.

But I don't put on a fake happy face

It's good if my outsides match my insides. If I'm not happy, I shouldn't try to look happy in an attempt to make others feels better.

My responsibility is to be authentically me—inside and outside. How other people react to my authenticity is their responsibility.

If my upset demeanor is off-putting to friends and family, I can, however, tell them what I'm feeling and why. Authentic mourning plus good communication equals empathy and support.

•

REFLECTION
I try to be authentic as I allow myself to mourn.

Sometimes understanding means standing under

As I work to befriend and understand my grief, I will at times realize that life and death contain many mysteries. I may not ever truly understand why someone I love had to die. I may not understand why life unfolds as it does.

Sometimes understanding grief means standing under the mysterious experience of human life and death. When this happens, I can choose to surrender my need for control and judgment. Surrender is not the same as giving up. Surrendering to the unknowable mystery is a courageous choice and an act of faith.

·

REFLECTION

I am in awe of and celebrate life's many mysteries.

I don't rely on alcohol or drugs to dull my pain

For many people it's tempting to avoid or mask the pain of grief with alcohol and drugs. This can lead to chemical dependence as well as unreconciled grief, which is a really harmful combination.

If I use chemicals, I do so in careful moderation. And if I'm having trouble with chemical abuse or dependence, I ask for help.

Instead of avoiding my pain, I encounter it authentically, in doses. Then when I need a break, I take a break from my grief in healthy ways.

•

REFLECTION

The pain of grief is a warning signal to not avoid my grief, but instead allow myself to experience it.

People with broken hearts deserve urgent care

If you're seriously wounded, you need immediate, practical, hands-on care. You head to urgent care because it's urgent. Or you rush to the emergency room because it's an emergency.

Yet many people with broken hearts try to ignore their injuries and continue on with their lives as best they can. They don't get immediate care. They don't seek first aid. It's a mistake that costs them the fullness of life.

I'm not making the same mistake.
I'm getting the help I need.

●

REFLECTION

Emotional and spiritual injuries require the same TLC as physical injuries.

I pull up a chair

When my grief comes knocking,
I open the door and I pull up a chair.

I sit with my grief when it needs company.
I offer it hospitality. And when I'm ready, I share
my grief outside of myself in some way.

Welcome, grief. I know you're actually love in
disguise. I would be a fool to turn you away.

•

REFLECTION
If I am inhospitable to grief,
I'm inhospitable to love.

I can continue a relationship if I choose

Since the death, I've had to come to terms with the fact that the person I love will never be physically present to me here on earth again. We can no longer be together. I hate it.

But many grieving people not only remember their loved ones who've died—they decide to continue a relationship with them in some way. Some talk out loud to their loved ones, sure they can hear them. Some imagine their loved ones live in heaven or a place that can't yet be comprehended, believing they will one day be reunited. Some write letters to the dead or visit the final resting place to continue to communicate with the person who died.

If I want to explore and cultivate some form of ongoing relationship, I can.

·

REFLECTION
I am always and forever connected
to the people I love.

I am not my mistakes

Everyone makes mistakes, including me.
I know I'm far from perfect.

I make mistakes in my grief, too.
If I'm hurting, I might lash out unfairly at others.
I treat myself badly. I stuff my grief inside me.
I say and do dumb things.

But despite it all, I am not my mistakes.
When I allow my inner wisdom to speak and act in
the world, my contributions have impact.
That is the true me.

·

REFLECTION
I think, speak, and act from the true me.

Not everyone had the privilege of waking up this morning

Since my loved one died, I might have had passing thoughts of wishing I wouldn't wake up again either. After all, the pain of grief is so sharp and deep and all-pervasive that it can be really hard knowing that every morning I'm going to reawaken to that painful reality.

But I'm also realizing that I'm still alive. Maybe I'm alive for a reason? And also, maybe it's a privilege to have woken up this morning. About 164,000 people worldwide did not.

My grief is terrible right now *and* it's a privilege to be alive. Those two truths exist side by side.

•

REFLECTION

This moment is a privilege.
So is this moment. And this one.

When I name my feelings, I tame my feelings

Part of acknowledging my feelings of grief is being aware of and naming them.

When I'm grieving, I'm often experiencing several feelings at once. I'm tempted to simply describe my feelings as "bad," "down," or "low." But when I sit with my feelings and really work to befriend them, I begin to see that I don't just feel "bad." For example, I might learn that in addition to sadness I actually feel a bit of disbelief, some anger, some regret, and a big dose of fear.

Discovering and naming my feelings in this way helps me understand each of them...and eventually reconcile them.

·

REFLECTION

I greet each of my feelings by name as they circle past. They are real but temporary visitors.

I remember other people who had a special relationship with the person who died

Often when people are naturally caught up in their own grief, they have a hard time empathizing with others grieving the same death. If this happens to me, I will know that it's normal.

But when I'm able, I'll take a look around me and notice that other people are grieving this death, too. I'm not alone.

If I reach out to these people, we can mourn together and comfort one another. What a relief and gift this can be.

•

REFLECTION

I know that I'm deeply connected to all of humanity.

The "firsts" are always hard

After a significant life loss, time stops. And eventually, it restarts. The earth keeps turning, the seasons pass, and we slowly return to regular activities and commitments.

The first time we return to a certain activity or event after a death is often difficult. The firsts that are hardest for me may be different than those of other mourners. The first grocery-store trip might be fine, but the first visit to a favorite restaurant might be painful. The first birthday, anniversary, or holiday is often heartbreaking.

I will be gentle and patient with myself as I encounter each first.

·

REFLECTION

If I'm dreading a first, I will not live in silent dread but instead express my thoughts and feelings to someone who cares about me.

Acceptance isn't enough

Acknowledging the reality of the loss is the first need of mourning. I'm learning to accept and allow that which I cannot control, because fighting the reality only causes me more suffering.

The further I journey into the wilderness of my grief, though, the more I realize that acceptance doesn't feel like enough. I want to do more with the death than accept it. I want to learn from it. I want to help other people in small but meaningful ways and make the world a better place. I want to carry my loved one's legacy forward.

Acceptance is an essential first step, but as long as I have the privilege of continuing to live, I have many more steps I can take.

·

REFLECTION

As I acknowledge the death, I allow myself to search for meaning.

I can make a grief kit

As I journey through my grief, I'm finding
that certain objects can help me access my grief or
comfort me when I need a dose of support.

I can gather up these objects and place them in a
special box or bag. Then, whenever I'm encountering
my grief, I can get out my grief kit
and readily find what I need.

Here are a few things I could put in my grief kit:
photos of the person who died and our life
together, souvenirs or other mementos, a candle
and matches, a journal and a pen, scented oils
whose fragrances remind me of the person who
died, a polished crystal or worry stone, a beautiful
book of poems or short readings.

•

REFLECTION
Anytime I want, I can access
objects from my grief kit.

I am finding a new normal

My life will never go back to the way it was. I will never be the same as I was.

There is no going back to the old normal. But I'm working on building a new normal. As I do so, it's important for me to remember that my new normal can be anything I want it to be.

If there were things about my old normal I didn't like, I have the power to change them. And the things about my old normal that I loved and am missing—well, those I am grieving. But even as I'm grieving and honoring what I've lost, I'm on the lookout for new possibilities to help fill in the gaps.

·

REFLECTION

Being at peace with whatever is—that's my new normal.

Of course I feel sad

Sadness is a natural, authentic emotion after the death of someone I love. Of course I feel deep sorrow. My sadness helps me slow down and take the time I need to reorder my life.

But I've noticed that other people are sometimes uncomfortable with my sadness. They tell me that the person who died wouldn't want me to be sad. They say that I should distract myself. They say I should think about what I still have to be thankful for.

I can't not be sad right now, though. It's where I am in my journey. And so I embrace my sadness, in doses, whenever I feel it tugging at me.

.

REFLECTION

When I'm mindful of the wonders of the present moment, my natural sadness is balanced by the miracle of living.

My life story unfolds in chapters

Like a book, my life story is broken up into chapters.
My childhood was a chapter. My teenage years
were a chapter. And then?

I'm realizing that where my chapters break depends not
only on my age and life stage but also on when major
changes and losses happen in my life. For instance,
committing to a partner starts a new chapter.
Moving to a new location starts a new chapter. And the
deaths of those closest to me also cause one chapter to
close and another to open.

I'm in a new chapter now. It's not one I was looking
forward to or maybe ever wanted to be in, but here I am.
So what will happen in this chapter…and the next?
There are many things I can't control, but I can work
to fill this chapter with as much presence, gratitude,
meaning, and purpose as possible.

·

REFLECTION

I choose love as the theme of my life story.

I'm taking my grief one day at a time

Grief is a long, arduous journey, and I can't predict where it's going. I can only trust that if I meet it openly and honestly each day, I will find the best path forward.

When I live in the now with my grief, and I express it in the now as it naturally arises, I am authentically mourning. Like the North Star, authentic, active mourning always points me in the right direction.

"Hello, grief," I say each morning. "What do you have to teach me today?"

·

REFLECTION
As much as possible, I live in the now.

Music helps me feel my feelings

Embracing my pain is necessary but oh so hard. I often want to avoid my pain or turn away from it.

Music helps by easing me into experiencing my pain. The right music summons my memories and my feelings of love and loss. It encourages me to allow my pain to wash over me. And it also supports me during these painful encounters. It's almost as if the sounds, the rhythms, and the words (if there are lyrics) provide a spiritual scaffold to hold me up.

I think I'll listen to some music today.

·

REFLECTION
Music speaks directly to my spirit.

I have hope for my grief journey

Hope is an expectation of a good that is yet to be. It is a forward-looking insight felt in the present moment.

I work on fostering hope for my future, but especially if I'm having trouble identifying with that type of hope right now, I can nurture hope for my grief journey itself.

I can hope that I'll authentically express my grief today. I can hope that I'll be kind to myself. I can hope that I'll connect with someone else in a meaningful way today, if only for a few minutes. I can hope that if I ever feel stuck, I'll reach out for help.

·

REFLECTION

I have hope for me and for you.

My body might express the stress of grief in lots of ways

The stress of grief can create tension and chemical reactions in my body.

In addition to causing sleep troubles and lethargy, the stress hormone cortisol can create inflammation, suppress my immune system, affect my digestion, cause aches and pains, elevate my heart rate, and raise my blood pressure.

To counteract the normal stress of grief, I'm actively using stress-management techniques that work for me.

·

REFLECTION

Whenever I feel stress, I immediately acknowledge it and then release it.

It's the missing that's the hardest

My grief challenges me in lots of ways, but missing the person who died is probably the hardest. The knowing that they're no longer here. The empty chair where they should be at the dinner table. The hand I can no longer hold. Instead of their presence, there's an emptiness. That emptiness is horrible. It can't be filled with anyone or anything else.

Yet I'm having to befriend the missing. I'm having to make the missing part of my ongoing life. It's so hard!

It helps to remember that the missing is love. And even though my precious person is no longer here for me to love in person, I can still talk about the love. I can still write about the love. I can still include the love in daily and special-day rituals. I can still act on the love.

·

REFLECTION

I continue to live and love deeply,
and I continue to miss you.

If I'm lonely, I'll seek connection

Loneliness in grief is common. Mourners often self-isolate, and friends—unsure of how to respond—fall away. The loss of a central relationship makes loneliness worse.

Some temporary loneliness in grief is normal. But profound and ongoing loneliness is harmful. Studies have shown that lonely people are more likely to get sick, suffer cognitive decline, and die sooner. Loneliness also triggers chronic inflammation, which heightens the risk of heart disease, stroke, and cancer.

If I'm feeling lonely, I'll know it's time to seek out connection. I will reach out to friends, family members, colleagues, neighbors, and acquaintances.

•

REFLECTION

Self-awareness and self-care create a "me" that is prepared to interact well with others.

I appreciate me

God knows I'm flawed. I'm just one imperfect human soul among the 108 billion who have ever walked this earth.

Right now especially, my life is a mess. I'm a mess. I don't know whether I'm coming or going. I don't know what I'm supposed to be doing.

But still, I appreciate me and my one singular, precious life. I'm living it as authentically and with as much meaning and purpose as I can.

·

REFLECTION

The embracing of grief makes me aware of the significance of my life. I can and will hold up this realization as my life continues to unfold.

I had no idea the pain could be this bad

Some losses hurt more than others. That's because a) some attachments are stronger than others, and b) some losses are just more traumatic (such as the death of a young person, deaths by suicide or homicide, accidental death, and others).

Before this loss, I thought I knew grief. After all, I'd experienced loss before. But this loss has me struggling profoundly. I had no idea the pain could be this bad or the journey this harrowing.

That's why I've turned to this book. I need a companion to help see me through.

·

REFLECTION

When I can't cope with my pain, I ask for help.

What if I chose to believe that all will be well?

Some people have faith that all will be well. They trust that no matter what hardships they, their loved ones, or the world are going through at this moment, eventually everything will be OK.

It was John Lennon who said, "Everything will be OK in the end. If it's not OK, it's not the end."

I can choose to believe this too, if I want. This belief wouldn't take away my need to grieve and mourn authentically right now, but it would be a beacon for me in the distance.

·

REFLECTION
I choose to remember that out of darkness eventually comes light.

I am not my loss and grief

When people are knocked over by a significant loss, they sometimes set up camp there. It's normal to be steamrolled by loss. And it's necessary to give my grief the time and attention it deserves.
But it's not normal or healthy to make my ongoing life only about loss and grief.

I am a multidimensional person with many facets. The relationship I had with the person who died may have been a very special, feature facet—but it was not the only one. As I'm grieving, I'm working on rebuilding my self-identity and exploring all my other facets.

I can both grieve and live. I can both mourn and find new meaning and purpose.

·

REFLECTION
My outer self-identity is not fixed but instead constantly changing. My true self-identity is not form-based but instead a timeless spirit.

I say I'm sorry

When I do something that hurts others,
I apologize as soon as possible.
When I have regrets, I express them,
and I say I'm sorry to anyone who may have
been harmed along the way.

My grief is teaching me that life is too short to live
with barriers between me and the people I care
about. And harmful words and deeds as well as
regrets often create such barriers.

The good news is that these barriers often fall
when two small words are spoken: I'm sorry.
They're so powerful, they're almost like a magic
spell. I wield them with abandon.

·

REFLECTION
When I act with presence and empathy,
I rarely hurt others.

I don't move on from my grief, I move forward with it

The idea of "moving on" from grief implies that mourners experience a loss then leave it behind them somehow.

But that's not how it works. How it works is we take our loss by the hand and learn to walk forward with it into our continuing lives.

I think of it like a snowball rolling down a hill. As I move through life, I pick up more and more experiences. They become part of me. I grow as I accommodate them.

·

REFLECTION

Every experience I've ever had is part of me.

I'm done taking things for granted

It's a hard lesson—learning that I didn't fully appreciate what I had until it was too late.

So now, to prevent this from happening again, I'm constantly bringing awareness to gratitude. What am I grateful for in this moment? What about now? And just as important—how can I express that gratitude? As I discover my gratitude, I'm erring on the side of full self-disclosure. If I love someone, I tell them. If I appreciate something, I say so.

I'm done taking things for granted. Instead, I'm making it a goal to live in constant appreciation.

•

REFLECTION

Awareness brings appreciation.

I cultivate resilience

Resilience is the capacity to bounce back after difficult life losses and transitions.

At the same time that I'm embracing my grief, I'm also cultivating my resilience. I'm not trying to "bounce back" in a phony, grief-avoiding way. Instead, I'm trying to focus on what I can control (mostly my own thoughts and actions) versus what I can't.

When I choose to think and act with kindness, love, hope, gratitude, and connection, I'm cultivating resilience.

•

REFLECTION
In allowing myself to be vulnerable, I discover I can also be resilient.

I might find a grief buddy

Though no one else will grieve this unique loss just as I do, there are lots of other people who've had similar experiences. No one can lead me through the wilderness of my grief, but there are fellow travelers.

If I haven't already, I might consider finding a grief buddy—someone who is also mourning a death— to talk to and share companionship with. We can call each other whenever one of us needs to talk. We can listen to each other without judgment. We can spend time together.

Sometimes one compassionate friend is all it takes.

·

REFLECTION
I support others, and they support me.

I must go backward before I can go forward

People tell me I need to move on. They tell me the person who died would want me to keep living my life. They act as if I can sever all ties with what has happened and look only forward.

Yet, grief by its very nature is a recursive process. That means it curves and spirals back on itself. It's repetitive. It covers the same ground more than once. In fact, it *requires* repetition to eventually soften and become reconciled.

I have to go backward, over and over again.

•

REFLECTION
Grief requires repetition.
I'll go backward as often as I need to.

I build bridges

The grief inside me is complex and shaped by lots of different things, including my past life experiences, my unique personality, and the relationship I had with the person who died. No one else can know all the nuances of my thoughts, feelings, and memories.

When I reach out for support from others, I know that they can't know everything. I don't expect them to. When I need to talk about a certain aspect of my grief or tell a story about the relationship or the death, I can build bridges of understanding, though. I try to convey enough information and background that my helpers better understand where I'm coming from. These bridges, in turn, facilitate empathy.

•

REFLECTION

Bridges help others cross over to me, and in their time of need, me to them.

I pay attention to what makes me feel strong

Many times my grief has made me feel helpless, lethargic, and unable. It knocks me down.

These feelings are normal. But as I befriend and express my grief, I'm experiencing more and more moments where I feel a spark of energy and strength.

Even as I'm grieving, I'm paying attention to these sparks, and I'm intentionally seeking out opportunities to kindle more of them.

·

REFLECTION

I attend to my divine spark in order to strengthen it.

When I dream about the person who died, I share these dreams with good listeners

Dreaming about the person who died is a way
to do the work of mourning.

My mind is struggling to make sense of what
happened. It also wants to know where the person
has gone. And it might be hung up on any unfinished
business I feel. Dreams help my mind work
on these conundrums.

It helps me to talk about my dreams with someone
who empathetically listens to what
I think the dreams mean, rather than tells me what
they think they mean. I might also have nightmares,
and if this happens, I especially need to talk them out.

•

REFLECTION
I welcome dreams as part of the mystery of life.

The wilderness of my grief is an uncharted wilderness

My grief is a creation of my unique self, the unique person who died, and the unique circumstances of both of our lives.

My wilderness of grief may be rockier or more level than those of others. I may find a straight path or, more likely, one full of unexpected twists and turns.

In my wilderness, I will encounter places that are meaningful only to me, and I will experience the topography in my own way.

·

REFLECTION

I celebrate my unique life and honor all of its twists and turns.

I'm discovering ways to cope

When I'm in pain, I need to be present to my pain, in doses. But it's really hard—being with pain. So I'm finding ways to make my pain more bearable.

I'm discovering the most effective ways for me to express my pain. Talking, writing, crying, screaming, art-making, praying— these are all possibilities.

I'm also discovering how to make sitting with my internal grief more tolerable. I'm being gentle with myself and finding things that comfort me. Spending time in nature might help, or hugging or caring for my companion animal.

·

REFLECTION
I've gained hard-won wisdom, and I'm reaching out to help others cope.

I can be a spiritual optimist

I can set my intention to be hopeful about reconciling my grief. Today and every day, I can choose to express my grief in ways that nurture meaning, hope, and connection with others.

While still acknowledging and honoring my dark emotions whenever they arise, I can also—at the same time—choose to be on the lookout for pessimism. When I become aware of its presence, I can bear witness to it and observe it as it falls away.

·

REFLECTION

I am a spiritual optimist. I attempt to enter each moment with openness and gratitude.

Sometimes denial saves me

Some realities are too much to take in all at once. Some losses are too great to bear as they occur.

That's where shock and denial come in. They protect me from being crushed by the weight of a terrible new reality. They help me live to grieve another day, and bit by bit they allow the door to open wider to allow in a little more of the reality.

Especially in the early days, shock and denial are my friends.

·

REFLECTION

The more I live in the present moment, the less I need denial to assist me. I'm learning that I'm capable of meeting most moments honestly and openly.

I have choices

My loss happened to me. I didn't choose it.
I didn't want it. And now I'm suffering the grief of
unwanted change.

But here, in my grief, I have lots of new choices. I
can choose to acknowledge, embrace, and express
my pain. I can choose to live mindfully and
meaningfully. I can choose to more actively look
for opportunities for gratitude.

Every moment, I have choices. I am waking up to
this realization.

•

REFLECTION
In each moment, I choose with awareness.

When people ask me how I'm doing, I tell them the truth

When friends and family members ask me how I'm doing, I no longer respond with "I'm fine" or "I'm doing pretty well" unless those statements are true. Mutual pretense helps no one.

Instead, I share something specific. "I cried this morning," I might say. Or, "The nights have been hard." Or, "I find myself worrying about the upcoming holiday."

When I'm specific and honest, I invite conversation and support. And I let others know that they can be honest about their feelings, too.

·

REFLECTION

I am a truth-teller when people ask how I am.

I watch out for displacing my grief

If I'm not befriending my grief openly, honestly, and fully, it might come out sideways.

If I'm irritable, bitter, or angry with other people, for example, those feelings might actually stem from my unencountered grief. If I'm distressed about other circumstances in my life and focusing on them instead of my grief, I might be displacing my grief.

Displaced grief is off-trail grief. If I notice it's happening, or if someone else is kind enough to suggest to me that it might be happening, I'll know it's time to get back on the healthy trail to healing.

·

REFLECTION

The more I learn to allow my deepest, most authentic emotions as they arise, the less apt I am to displace them with surface feelings.

I try to remember that everyone suffers

When I'm hurting, I sometimes feel like other people have it easier. I experienced a major loss, and they haven't. It can feel like life isn't fair.

It's true that life isn't equitable. But it's also true that everyone suffers along the way. Almost no one makes it through life without experiencing great losses and hardships.

So when I'm feeling envious of certain people or families whose lives seem perfect, I'll remember this. They, too, have probably suffered in the past, and they will again in the future. And they're likely fighting battles right this minute that I know nothing about.

Sharing my understandable feelings of injustice and envy with a good listener will also help me through them.

•

REFLECTION
Proper sorrows of the soul are parts
of the human experience.

I am humbled by grief

There's nothing like loss and grief to make a person feel humble. Since the death of someone I love, I'm reminded that I'm not really in charge of my life or anyone else's. I may get to decide what happens in small ways, but when it comes to the huge issues of life and death, I'm not in control.

When I approach my grief from a place of humility, I allow it to teach me. I learn to follow it wherever it takes me. I surrender to its wisdom.

Humility in grief also means remembering that other people have their own grief stories and hard-won wisdom. I can learn from them, too, and should exercise caution when I venture to share my grief "expertise."

●

REFLECTION
I value humility over expertise.

Mending my broken heart may be the most worthy goal I've ever set for myself

When a broken heart goes uncared-for,
it can ruin your life.

Many mourners lock up their broken hearts and throw away the key. They mistakenly believe that if they're "strong" and "carry on," they can more or less ignore their broken hearts and move forward anyway.

The trouble is, it doesn't work like that. When brokenhearted people choose to remain stuck in denial or numbness, they die while they are alive. And they rarely realize what's happening to them. I want better for myself. I want to open my grieving heart and work on healing.

·

REFLECTION
I move toward instead of away from
challenging thoughts and feelings.

My grief is organic

I know that grief is normal and necessary. But even more than that, I'm finding, it's organic. It arises of its own accord. It ebbs and flows in its own time. It just happens, and as it does, it shifts and changes naturally, following its own mysterious path.

If I can ignore the cultural norms that try to tell me that my grief is bad or shameful or weak, I see that it's actually one-hundred-percent natural.

When I see my grief as organic and instinctive, my feelings toward it change. I'm more receptive to it and better able to befriend it. Like a forest wilderness, my grief is a wondrous natural force.

·

REFLECTION

Selfless love is organic. So too is the grief that emanates from that love.

Feelings of relief and release in grief are normal

There are good reasons why grieving people sometimes feel a sense of relief or release after the death of someone loved. If the death followed a difficult illness, for example, or if the person who died suffered from mental illness or addiction, it's natural for the grief of those left behind to be tinged with some degree of relief.

Feelings of relief are normal in grief, and if I feel them, that's OK. They don't equate to callousness or a lack of love for the person who died.

My grief contains whatever it contains. Everything belongs.

·

REFLECTION

I'll be well-served to remember—relief is not about a lack of love. It is often an expression of love.

I experience the sacred

When I encounter a sacred moment or experience, I know it. I feel that glow of profound meaningfulness. I have an "aha" sensation that life is not only good, it's timeless and more spiritual than I can understand.

Sometimes I encounter the sacred by happenstance. I glimpse a flower or gaze into a smiling child's face, and I'm suddenly transported to a deeper connection with the divine. And sometimes I'm wise and go in search of the sacred. I seek out places, people, and activities that foster that same feeling of connection and wonder deep inside me.

In these special moments, I get a peek at the spirit world. In these special moments, I glimpse the understanding that life and death are part of the same timeless continuum.

·

REFLECTION

As much as possible,
I find the sacred in every moment.

When I feel like crying, I cry

Tears of grief aren't a weakness—
they're a superpower.

Crying emotional tears releases stress chemicals
from the body. I feel better after I cry. Crying also
alerts others to the fact that I'm upset and could
use some empathetic support.

Tears of grief are a sacred gift. They communicate
both my love and my heartbreak.

·

REFLECTION
I'm not afraid to express my true
feelings through tears.

I can choose not to engage

When other people misunderstand my grief,
offer bad advice, or judge me for not "moving on,"
I can try to educate them, or I can
choose not to engage.

Sometimes I might feel like teaching a close
friend or loved one about the reality of my grief
and how they can and cannot support me
best—and sometimes I might not.

I must first direct my energy to authentic
mourning and self-care. I also have to take care
of my daily commitments. If I don't have enough
energy or interest left over to be a grief ambassador,
that's OK. I'm doing what I need to do.

·

REFLECTION

I engage in the world in ways that promote
kindness and mindful presence.

I have good relationships with healthcare providers

Part of my grief self-care means taking
good care of my body.

And part of my bodily care is having a team
of healthcare providers who know me and are
available to support me. In addition to a primary
healthcare provider, I might work with a massage
therapist, a nutritionist, a chiropractor, a wellness
coach, a personal trainer, and/or other specialists.

I don't need to over-rely on care providers, but
I should feel good about proactively seeking the
care I need to take care of myself and
stave off any serious troubles.

·

REFLECTION

My body reminds me that it requires my attention.

I'm rethinking my priorities

It's funny, but some of the things that used to be important to me aren't so much anymore.

I find myself rethinking my assumptions, values, and priorities. I might be questioning my religious or spiritual values. I might be reexamining my relationships with material goods, status, appearances, and money.

I'm changing, and some of my priorities are changing. That's a normal part of grief.

•

REFLECTION

Belongings don't matter. Status doesn't matter.
People and relationships matter.

I try again

My grief journey is rocky and unpredictable.
I don't know how I'm going to feel from one day
to the next, and even though I'm practicing good
self-care and actively mourning, I sometimes feel
like I'm slipping backward into despair.

So I try again. I sit with my grief and befriend it
again. I express whatever it is I'm feeling again.
I reach out for love and support again.

Grief can definitely be a one-step-forward, two-
steps-backward process. Still, I know that in
general, working on the six needs of mourning
will carry me in the right direction. So I try again.

·

REFLECTION
I'm not discouraged. I am encouraged.

There is life in grief

One of the most poignant realizations about grief is that it's for the living. It may be caused by death (and other major losses), but it's a living, breathing, here-on-earth, in-the-now human experience.

Which means that there is life in grief! In fact, it's brimming with the most heartfelt emotions and actions life has to offer.

I only grieve because I love.
And I love and grieve because I'm alive.

·

Part of being human is to love and to grieve.

I look for signs

Some grieving people look for clues that the person who died is communicating with them in some way. I can look for and believe in these signs if I want to. They help many grievers find a sense of hope and peace.

But I can also look for other kinds of signs. For example, I can be on the alert for signs that other people care about me. I can watch for signs that my grief is softening and changing. I can look for signs that direct me to meaning and purpose in my daily life.

·

REFLECTION

To look for signs is to be alive to life's possibilities.

I'm growing stronger

At first I felt my grief was so large that it would completely crush me. I would be pulverized into a million pieces, never to survive.

But then I survived. And I began to befriend my grief. And slowly and over time, it seemed to get smaller.

But then I realized: It's not so much that my grief is getting smaller. I'm getting bigger. I'm gaining the wisdom and strength of one who has loved and lost, and is working to integrate the loss. It's not wisdom and strength that I asked for or wanted. No, there's no question I'd rather have my loved one back. But nonetheless, here I am, growing stronger.

·

REFLECTION

Strength lies not in defeating life's challenges
but in befriending them.

Hope is like a seedling

Spring is the season of new beginnings. It's when life reawakens. Bare tree branches bud, and tiny green seedlings emerge from the cold, black ground.

Depending on how long ago my loss took place and how traumatic it was for me, I may or may not feel like it's time for new beginnings. I may or may not be ready for my life to reawaken.

But regardless, I can be watchful for any tiny seedlings of hope that emerge. When I notice them—regardless of when they appear—I'll know that the spring of my grief is possible. If I continue to nurture those seedlings, they'll grow stronger and more vigorous, and the day will come when they will burst into bloom.

•

REFLECTION
I'm present with love and gratitude,
and I'm hopeful about the future.

I intend to live wholeheartedly

As I feel my tender, broken heart slowly mending, I find I'm charting a course to live deeply again.

I don't intend to live halfheartedly. I intend to live wholeheartedly. This will take courage, compassion, and connection.

Courage—to be vulnerable, to take risks and reach for what I really, truly want and care about. Compassion—to see the good in everyone and to care for myself with loving tenderness. And connection—to actively participate in life through meaningful relationships.

·

REFLECTION

As I heal my broken heart, I need caring people who continue to support and understand me.

I go backward to heal old griefs

As I go backward before moving forward, I may encounter past, unreconciled griefs. It's normal for new grief to bring up old grief.

I am learning that any pain that is left unhealed, and any unfinished business that is never explored, can destroy my enthusiasm for life and living. They can extinguish my divine spark. They can deny me my creativity, gifts, and talents.

If I discover old griefs I am carrying, I will get help to mourn them and lay them down.

·

REFLECTION

When I'm open to whatever each day brings, I don't deny or skip over anything. I meet it as it comes.

My patchwork heart craves meaning

My healing heart has hard-won wisdom.
It's where my divine spark lives.
It's the seat of my soul.

My healing heart craves wonder, joy, gratitude,
congruence, and meaning.

I can tell when a belief or value I hold is heart-created because it's grounded in empathy and love. Ego-created beliefs and values, on the other hand, are grounded in judgment and fear. My heart is by far the wiser.

·

REFLECTION
I choose empathy and love.

I'm kind to myself

I'm wounded, and I need tender loving care. I need it from others, and I need it from myself.

So I'm kind to myself. I'm self-compassionate, patient, and understanding.

When I don't meet expectations—mine or others'—for how I'm doing with my grief, that's OK. I accept myself, and I love myself. As much as possible, I take good care of myself.

·

REFLECTION
In loving myself, I prepare myself to love others and life.

I sometimes lose control

Sometimes powerful emotions overwhelm me,
and I feel out of control. I may get hysterical or sob
or laugh uncontrollably. I may have angry outbursts.
I might say or do rash things.

While I'm working to befriend my feelings
in the moment and greet them calmly and
compassionately, occasionally they grab the wheel,
and for a short period of time I'm powerless to steer.

When this happens, it's OK. It's normal to be
overwhelmed by life's heartbreaks sometimes.
In these moments, I may need help from
a kind but strong helper.

·

REFLECTION

My feelings don't control me, and I don't control them.
Instead, my feelings flow through me.

I understand the difference between support and toxic positivity

I need and deserve the support of others as I journey through grief. In fact, receiving this support is my sixth need of mourning. But I'm realizing that there's a difference between genuine empathetic support and fake toxic support.

Genuine supporters create a safe place for me to feel and express my grief and to share my story of love and loss. They listen and validate without judgment or the need to give advice.

Fake supporters, on the other hand, may look like supporters on the outside, but they're actually toxic. The people who tell me that I'm strong and will get over it, or that I just need to keep my chin up and think happy thoughts, are dismissing my very real need to be sad and mourn.

•

REFLECTION
I appreciate genuine support.

I meet up with friends at least once a week

Receiving ongoing support from others is
one of my needs of mourning. So I facilitate
this by making sure I spend time with
friends at least once a week.

This doesn't happen by accident. It's easy for weeks to
slide by without friends getting together.

That's why I plan it. I reach out, and I schedule simple
get-togethers, like coffee dates and walks in the park.
If I'm unable to get together in-person,
I can schedule a phone call.

Fostering relationships not only gives me
opportunities to talk about my loss, it also strengthens
the bonds that make life worth living.

•

REFLECTION

I crave connection, and I indulge those healthy cravings.

I'm patient with my slow movement toward accepting the reality of the death

Acknowledging the reality of the death of someone I love is slow, painful work. At first I come to acknowledge it with my head, but it takes longer to acknowledge it with my heart.

It's normal to push away the reality sometimes. I might immerse myself in activities that help me avoid the reality. This gives me a necessary break from my pain, but I know that I also have to find ways to move toward the reality, one small step at a time.

I'm patient with myself as I work on accepting the reality of the death.

·

REFLECTION

I'm getting better at accepting difficult realities as they arise. I flow with life.

It's OK to step away from thoughts that are pulling me under

Certain things about the death are especially hard for me to think about and feel. I know that moving toward my grief instead of away from it is what I need to do on my journey to healing, but sometimes a thought pulls me under.

When this happens, it's a sign that I need a break from my grief. I step away and do something else.

When it's time to encounter that same thought again, I'll reach out for support. I'll talk to a friend or fellow mourner, I'll go to a support-group meeting, or I'll visit a grief counselor. I need help befriending the hardest things.

·

REFLECTION

I'll remember my mind serves my spirit, not the other way around.

There's peace in forgiveness

During my grief journey, I might get stuck in any number of thoughts and feelings.
A common one is anger.

Anger is a perfectly fine and normal thing to feel. But the more I explore and befriend my anger, the more I see that it might be mixed up with or masking other feelings, like regret, guilt, and despair.

Whatever it is I'm angry about, I can choose to move toward forgiveness if I want to. My anger causes me to suffer. In forgiveness, I may discover less suffering and more peace.

•

REFLECTION
When I don't judge, I don't have to forgive.

Imagine that

In some ways my loss has woken me up.
It's a steep price to pay for awareness,
but that's what's happened.

Now, with my newfound awareness, I see all
the miracles around me more readily. And I'm
also noticing that all of the objects and systems
that comprise my life were once the product of
someone's imagination. I look around my house
and think, "None of this used to exist."

I, too, have the power of imagination. I can think
of new things, experiences, and circumstances
that don't yet exist. And for those that resonate
with meaning and purpose, I can work toward
bringing them to life in ways small or large.

•

REFLECTION
I imagine, and I bring forth.

I'm seeking reconciliation, not resolution

I won't "get over" my grief. It will never truly end.

Instead, my loss experience will become an integral part of who I am. My story of love and loss will be featured in the tapestry of my life.

I can't resolve my grief, but I can reconcile it. I can integrate it into my life as I find ways to live the rest of my days with meaning and purpose.

•

REFLECTION
I do not resist. Instead, I allow. Everything belongs.

If I ever lose hope, I can borrow it

Try as I might to be intentional and proactive about nurturing hope, I sometimes just can't. There are days when I might feel nothing but despair.

When I feel hopeless, though, I have a fallback plan in place. My plan is to reach out to others whom I know have hope to spare.

Some people are just good at helping me feel more hopeful. Some are empathetic listeners, and simply talking about my grief can help ease my sense of hopelessness. Others are survivors of a similar loss, and their wisdom about how it gets better can rekindle my hope. And still others are happy, joyful people. Spending time with them can lift my spirits. I can borrow hope from all of them.

·

REFLECTION

I'm a hope lender and receiver.

Emotional pain is a normal part of human life

Our "don't-worry-be-happy" culture pretends that happiness is the status quo. It teaches us that happiness and contentment should be the norm and that pain and strife are the aberrations.

Unfortunately, that's just not true. In this age of disinformation, that's one of the biggest falsehoods of all.

Life is constant change, and change is often painful. Acknowledging this and learning how to live authentically in and through times of painful change are, in large part, what I'm working on.

•

REFLECTION

I don't resist but instead surrender to the normal pain of life.

I'm putting it all out there

My loss has made me aware of the brevity of life.
There's no time to waste.

So when I really want to do something, I do it.
I don't wait for a special occasion. Today is the
special occasion, and I might not
have another one.

This means I have to take some chances.
It means I have to risk making mistakes.
But if I don't put it all out there, I may die with
unsung songs inside me. And that would be
an unconscionable shame.

·

REFLECTION
As Helen Keller said, "Life is a daring
adventure or nothing at all."

The circumstances of a death shape my grief

How a loved one dies affects my grief. How old a loved one is when they die affects my grief.

The more traumatic the death circumstances, the more traumatic my grief.

If I'm struggling with the circumstances of a death, I deserve—and sometimes may need—extra help, including the support of a professional counselor, to move toward reconciling my grief.

•

REFLECTION
Life is chaotic change. There are times
I need and deserve support.

Grief is my shadow

My grief is dark. It can loom large. It's always connected to me. It follows me wherever I go.

When I allow myself to step into the warm afternoon sunshine of awareness and friendship, my grief shadow falls in front of me, where I can see it and talk to it.

That's when I know that my grief *is* me—not all of me but a big part of me. It's not scary or foreboding. I think I will wave hello.

•

REFLECTION
I hold both love and grief by the hand.

God can handle my anger and doubts

My loss might have me questioning my faith. It might make me angry, frustrated, or sad about God's role in my life. This doesn't mean I'm being "weak" in my faith. On the contrary, it means I have a relationship with God or a higher power that's strong enough to withstand honesty and exploring feelings.

If I belong to a religious group, I don't let them take away my natural and necessary grief in the name of faith. Faith and mourning are not mutually exclusive. Actually: "Blessed are those who mourn, for they shall be comforted."

•

REFLECTION

I explore my spirituality freely, with an open mind and an open heart.

I'm not crazy—
I'm grieving

My grief can sometimes make me feel
like I'm losing it. I can be so forgetful, mixed up,
emotional, tearful, and "not myself."
I feel like I'm going crazy.

But I'm not crazy. I'm grieving.

Loss and grief are such disruptive life experiences
that they create a lot of normal chaos in both
my internal and external realities. I'll naturally
experience a period of chaos—likely for months—
before things begin to settle down again.

·

REFLECTION
There are times in life that disorientation
precedes reorientation.

I think I'll take a walk

When I feel stuck in my pain, lethargy, or certain anxious thought patterns (which may or may not reflect the truth), I can go for a walk. It doesn't have to be a long walk. Maybe I commit to walking for just five minutes. Outside, in the fresh air, is best, but indoors works too.

These little walks are like a reboot on my computer. They reset me. The physical activity circulates my blood, oxygenates my brain, and boosts my happy neurochemicals, like serotonin and dopamine. And if I'm in nature, those positive effects are compounded.

Putting my grief into motion gives it a tiny jolt of momentum.

·

REFLECTION
My body thrives on movement,
so I move it daily as I am able.

There's a chasm between my old life and my new one

My old life was on one side of a vast canyon,
and my new life is on the other side.
I'm in the chasm in between.
"Help! I'm stuck down here!" I want to shout.

My grief journey is all about getting from one side
to the other. It's a challenging trek, to say the least.
Other people can help me, but they can't carry
me. They can walk beside me now and then.

I can't yet see what the other side will look like.
But I know it's there, waiting for me. I can see the
edge of it in the distance. So I keep going.

•

REFLECTION

It's OK that I'm in a place between
my past and my future.

I look for kinship

When we say the word "kin," we usually
mean biological family. Blood relatives.
But kinship also means sharing meaningful
characteristics or origins.

Kinship in grief comes from building relationships
and mutual support systems with other grievers.
Not everyone can understand and empathize
with my profound grief, but often, people
who've experienced a similar loss can.

When I'm building my support system, I look for
kinship. Right now, these are my truest soulmates.

·

I'm well-served to remember: I need not walk alone.

I'm finding ways to use my potential

I have gifts and passions. I'm naturally good at certain things, and I'm drawn to certain things. As I work on developing my new self-identity, I'm paying particular attention to my gifts and passions.

What have I always wanted to do but haven't yet done? What am I doing right now that I don't particularly enjoy or feel good about? What am I good at? How can I help others using my gifts and talents?

These are the kinds of questions I'm asking myself. I'm trying new things as I search for fulfilling answers.

·

REFLECTION

Maintaining a positive mindset helps me discover and use my potential.

Messy is just fine

Let's just call it like it is:
Grief and mourning are messy.

It can be loud and unruly. It can be lethargic and scroungy. It can be forward then backward. It can be up then down. And it can be all of those things (and many more) within the same day!

My grief journey isn't beautiful and well-organized. You couldn't Pinterest it. But I'm trying to make sure it's authentic. And that's all that really matters.

·

REFLECTION
I understand that grief often brings
chaos and confusion.

I pay it forward

As I receive kindness and support in my grief journey, I'm grateful. And when I'm feeling ready, I remember to pay it forward.

I can pay kindness and support forward in lots of ways, big and small. Saying hello with a smile to a stranger is paying it forward. So is calling a friend out of the blue, volunteering, sharing financial good fortune, and performing any random act of kindness.

Whenever I pay it forward, I give a gift and I get a gift. I feel an immediate sense of satisfaction and connection with humanity.

•

REFLECTION
What I put forth is what I receive.

I nurture my divine spark

Deep inside me is my divine spark—
that which gives my life meaning and purpose.
It's the still, small voice inside me that guides me
to meaning and purpose.

My divine spark is my spiritual self.
It's the deepest, truest me.

Whether or not I'm religious, I understand
the importance of nurturing my spirit as
often as possible.

·

REFLECTION

As I allow myself to mourn, I have the
capacity to relight my divine spark.

There is no cure for grief, but there is care for grief

My grief can't be cured. First of all, there's nothing wrong with me. I'm not ill. I don't have a disorder or condition. Second, my grief can't be magically fixed. Nothing can make it go away. In fact, it will always be part of me.

But there *is* care for my grief! I care for it by actively engaging with the six needs of mourning in doses and by taking good, kind care of myself physically, cognitively, emotionally, socially, and spiritually.

Actually, now that I think about it, I realize that the only real "cure" for any of life's many challenges is tender loving care.

·

REFLECTION

I care for myself well so that I can be present to care for others well.

I am a singular creation

There's only one me. There's never been another just like me, and there never will be again.

I am a once-in-infinity miracle.

This means that all by myself, independent of all of my relationships with other people in life, including the person who died, I am a unique and special child of the universe/God. Even though I'm just little old me, I am also individually amazing. I'm working on getting to know me again and living out my uniqueness.

•

REFLECTION

This soul inside me shines.

I focus on the journey, not the destination

Just as love is best experienced in the moment, grief—love's twin—is most authentically experienced in the moment as well.

When I'm befriending and expressing my grief as it naturally arises, I'm authentically living my grief journey. I'm not worrying so much about where I'm headed or how long it's going to take to get there. Instead, I'm inhabiting the now of my grief.

The funny thing is, living in the now of my grief plus a smattering of intention, gratitude, nature, and ritual is the best roadmap to get me where I want to go. So I immerse myself in the journey and trust the destination will take care of itself.

·

REFLECTION
The journey is all there ever is.

I regularly exercise my body

I've learned that I can mourn more effectively when my body is well-rested and well taken care of.

Regular exercise isn't optional. It's as essential as breathing, sleeping, and eating.

I don't need to be a hardcore athlete or gym fanatic to get enough exercise, though. A thirty-minute walk, bike ride, or physical chore most days of the week is enough.

•

REFLECTION

I treat my body with respect and kindness.

I can be silly

Moments of humor and levity in grief remind me
that everything's not doom and gloom.
Human life may be full of difficult loss and
change, but it's also funny.

So I give myself permission to be silly.
I look for opportunities to chuckle and have fun.
I spend time in the company of people who know
how to have a good time and who make me laugh.
Children, especially, make great company
when I need a dose of silly.

How can I carve out some silly time today?

·

REFLECTION
Laughter makes everything better.

What if my heart breaks again?

It will.

As I continue to live, my heart will almost certainly be broken again. The globe spins. The years pass. And things continue to change.

But the next time my heart breaks, I will be better prepared. I will know better how to grieve and mourn effectively. I will know better how to create momentum toward a renewed life of meaning and purpose.

It will still hurt. Knowing what to do with the hurt doesn't prevent the hurt. But it will make the hurt more of a friend.

·

REFLECTION

When my heart breaks, I know the only way to the other side is through.

I nurture hope

Hope is an expectation of a good that is yet to be.
It's an expression of the present alive
with a sense of the possible.

Hope is a forward-looking insight experienced in
the now. It's an essential part of healthy mourning
and healing. In the now, I nurture hope by
honoring the ten touchstones and actively and
intentionally mourning.

I also nurture hope by paying attention to
whatever sparks hope in me. Some activities and
self-care habits make me feel hopeful. Spending
time with certain people makes me feel hopeful.
I schedule these bits of hope into each day.

·

REFLECTION
I try to find hope in each moment, and I share my
hope with others who may need to borrow it.

Whatever I feel, it's OK

My grief feelings are not right or wrong—
they simply *are*.

If I notice I'm feeling ashamed of any of my
feelings, it's probably because I've internalized the
misconception that some feelings are bad.
I'm learning that's not true.

Others may try to shame me for or dissuade me
from certain feelings, too. I'll seek out listeners who
accept my feelings as they are, instead.

·

REFLECTION

In large part, my feelings flow from mindless thoughts.
When I'm mindful and truly inhabiting the moment,
I experience feelings of peace and gratitude.

I triage my grief

Triage means taking a close, honest look
at my loss injury and determining what
needs to be done to care for it.

1. I acknowledge that I'm experiencing grief.

2. I take stock of and name the symptoms
   I'm having.

3. I allow myself to feel and express the
   symptoms.

I do these three steps over and over,
for as long as it takes.

•

REFLECTION

I take a look at my grief and give it the attention
it needs and deserves.

If my natural depression becomes clinical depression, I'll get help

There is a natural depression in grief. Grief forces me to slow down and turn inward. It dulls my ability to find pleasure in life. It makes me feel sad and also empty sometimes.

But if I find that I'm having trouble functioning in my daily life, I may be clinically depressed. Other signs of clinical depression include persistent low self-esteem and apathy.

If I think I might be clinically depressed, if I've been having thoughts of suicide, or if others tell me they're concerned about my depression, it's time to make an appointment with my primary care provider.

They will help me get the help I need.

•

REFLECTION

When I need help, I recognize it and seek it without hesitation.

I celebrate the freedom to mourn

It turns out that openly and authentically expressing my grief is a freedom to celebrate.

I don't have to bottle everything up inside me! I don't have to be silent! What a relief it is to be expressive and honest!

In psychology speak, congruency means being on the outside who I am on the inside, especially when it comes to the things that matter the most to me. In grief, being congruent feels so much better, and I can tell that it's helping me heal.

•

REFLECTION
I celebrate life.

I can try acting "as if"

I'm all about being authentic in grief. I've learned that if I'm not honest, I can't get any momentum toward healing. But once in a while I need a little push. I might get stuck in a self-sabotaging rut, and none of my honest mourning efforts seem to be helping. That's when I can try acting "as if."

In cognitive behavioral therapy, clients are sometimes taught to act as if they already are what they want to be. In essence, they role play.

Let's say I'm feeling insecure and incapable. I can pretend I'm a self-assured, confident person. I can act as if I'm brave.

·

REFLECTION

Sometimes acting "as if" helps me regain the healthy momentum I need.

I deserve to heal

Some days I can't even imagine getting through this. But then I remember: I deserve to heal. I deserved to have great love in my life, and now I deserve to find my way through my grief and back to fully living and loving.

It's the daily work of active mourning that will get me from here to there. For now I must trust that engaging with one or more of the six needs of mourning each day—in doses—will give me the momentum I need to move toward healing.

No matter what happens in my life, I deserve kindness, love, and healing.

•

REFLECTION
While grief and mourning unfold slowly,
I can set my intention to eventually heal.

The "right time"? There's no such thing

In grief it can be hard to know when the time is right to take a step toward life without the person who died.

How much time should pass before I donate clothing or clean out the hobby equipment? When is it OK to take a vacation or relocate? Is there a rule of thumb for the recommended grief period before dating again, trying to have or adopt another child, etc.?

It's normal to wonder, but the truth is that the "right" answer is only what's right for me. As long as I'm not rushing myself in an attempt to go around my grief, I'll know that when I feel deeply, confidently ready, the time is right for me.

•

REFLECTION

I allow my intuition to guide me in each moment.

I move from resentment to acceptance

It's normal to resent certain aspects of grief and loss.
I don't want it. It's not fair. I sometimes feel bitter,
annoyed, or angry.

So I sit with my resentment, and I let it teach me.
I express it by talking with others about it, too. And
eventually, over time, it starts to soften.

As it attenuates, I come to realize that I can transition
from resentment to acceptance. I then see that I can
choose peace, love, and forgiveness instead.
And when I radiate peace, love, and forgiveness,
I get back more peace, love, and forgiveness in return.
Staying stuck in resentment closes me off from these
life-affirming experiences.

•

REFLECTION
Hanging on to resentment serves little purpose.

I'm aware that obsessions can be a sign of off-trail grief

Sometimes grieving people distract themselves with various obsessions to the point that they ignore their grief. Overworking is a good example of this. Shopping, over-exercising, gambling, video gaming, and other addictive behaviors are other examples. Crusading about something related to the loss can be another.

Any all-consuming passion or behavior that distracts me from authentically embracing and expressing my grief—much of the time and for a long period of time—is likely a sign of off-trail grief.

If I'm off-trail, I'll get some extra help. Seeing a good grief counselor is a way to get back on track.

·

REFLECTION
While I may get off-trail in my grief,
I can always get back on-trail.

It's good to slow down

Whenever possible, I choose to live
life in the slow lane.

Slowing down the pace of my life helps me more
authentically experience and express my grief.
When I'm less distracted and more present, I can
better embrace my grief and mourn, as well as
experience wonder and joy.

The quality of my life is determined not by
how many things I do or accomplish in a day
but instead by how present I am no matter
what is happening.

·

REFLECTION
In each moment, I try to appreciate
the joy of simply being.

I may be growing, but it's not growth I'd choose

People say that our greatest gifts
come from our wounds.

Ultimately, that statement may or may not be
true. But even if I've gained gifts since my loss,
I'd rather have the person who died back—
whole, healthy, and happy.

Loss is not a gift or a blessing. Sometimes
I appreciate the gifts and growth I've experienced
since the loss. And sometimes they feel like
entirely unwanted, inadequate recompense.
It's OK for me to see them as both.

·

REFLECTION

While I don't seek out wounds, when I experience
them I try to learn from them.

Even tiny pebbles cause ripples

As I work on the six needs of mourning, sometimes it feels like my small efforts aren't making a difference.

If I have a short chat with a friend about my loss, or if I cry for a few minutes, I might not feel any better. But over time, I notice that even my brief mourning stints are adding up to help give me momentum.

That chat with a friend can easily turn into an invitation to get together for dinner next week. That little cry helped reinforce that crying is OK. Every little pebble of mourning ripples out into my life in ways that carry me.

•

REFLECTION

Small, daily efforts are more effective than infrequent heroics.

I have things to share with the world

I'm still here. Why am I still here?

Maybe it's because I still have things to share with the world. I have things to do, people to help, places to go. I have unique gifts and talents that are not yet fully explored or tapped.

Today I will intentionally share something of myself, in some small way, and I will notice how it feels.

.

REFLECTION

I'm an integral part of the dance of human life.

Grief lasts a lifetime

When a love of my life dies, I know that
my grief, too, will last a lifetime.

A grief is as powerful and enduring as the love it's
coupled with. As the poet Kahlil Gibran famously
wrote, "When you are sorrowful, look again in your
heart, and you will see that in truth you are weeping
for that which has been your delight."

I'm befriending my sorrow, trusting that over time
this will help it soften. But it is now a part of me
forever, just as my love is a part of me forever.

·

REFLECTION
My loves and my wounds are part of me.

How others behave is about them, not about me

As I journey through the wilderness of my grief,
I need people to walk alongside me in support.
But sometimes the people in my life make
my journey even harder.

When people judge me or direct their rage, irritation,
or envy at me, or try to make me feel guilty or
unworthy in some way, I try to remember that their
behavior is really about them—not about me.

People who are being cruel, unfair, or negative toward
me usually have deep-seated internal issues with self-
esteem and fear. I can choose to acknowledge this and
walk away, or I can show mercy and offer empathy in
return. Either way, it's not about me.

·

REFLECTION
I see and bless the humanity in each person.

I love my life in the here and now

I'm grieving the loss of a life that is over. But one of the ironies of grief is that while it's giving me a newfound appreciation for all the little moments I got to share with that person, it's also distracting me from all the little moments I'm experiencing right now.

My task is to befriend my grief and actively mourn so I can be as present to my ongoing life as possible.

When I love my life in the here and now, I do the most honor to the person who died. They are physically gone, but I am privileged to still be here. I bring my love and grief for them with me into each new moment, and I experience all of it together.

·

REFLECTION

I'm constantly returning my wandering heart to the now.

I'm a mistake maker

Boy, am I imperfect. I make so many mistakes!

But I'm glad I make mistakes, because it means I'm
trying. If I didn't put myself out there,
I wouldn't have the chance to make mistakes.
I'd be playing it safe, but I would also be
dying while I was alive.

So here's to the mistake makers and the chance takers.
We're truly living this life.

·

REFLECTION
There are no real mistakes, just teachable moments.

I'm befriending impermanence

It's not just grief I'm befriending.
I'm befriending impermanence.

I'm surrendering to the reality that nothing
stays the same. Over the course of a human lifetime,
some people die and others are born. Friendships
begin and end. Partnerships form and dissolve.
Living situations are in constant flux.

So it's not just this loss I'm surrendering to. I'm
also yielding to the understanding that the other
attachments in my life are also impermanent. Instead
of constantly thinking about what's to come (I don't
know!), I'm focusing on the now, which is itself
fleeting but is also the only certainty I ever have.

•

REFLECTION
Acknowledging my mortality allows me to
live more fully in the present.

I spend time in nature to enhance my healing

Nature is a healer.

It's restorative and energizing to spend time outside. There's something calming and awe-inspiring about walking, biking, gardening, or simply sitting in a natural setting. Afterwards, I return to my indoor environment feeling rested and refreshed.

I can also bring nature inside. Houseplants, natural foods, and aromatherapy are just a few easy ways to incorporate nature into my home life.

•

REFLECTION

I try to spend time almost every day experiencing and feeling one with nature.

My grief is heart-based

Grief is primarily an emotional and spiritual
journey. While I can and do think about my loss,
I cannot reason my way out of grief. And not
everything I experience as part of my normal grief
is rational or "makes sense."

The word "courage" comes from *coeur*,
the Old French word for heart. I am mustering the
courage to deeply and authentically feel
and honor my grief.

I'm also learning that it's easier and quicker
to understand the fact of a death with my head.
Only over time and through befriending
my grief am I coming to truly understand
the loss with my heart.

·

REFLECTION

I courageously live my life, love, and grief heart first.

I look to my intuition

Through grief I've become more attuned to my emotions and my spirit. I'm paying more attention to my gut feelings and reactions.

When I'm trying to decide next steps or make choices, I look to my intuition. It's listening deeply with my heart, my soul, my mind, and even my body.

My intuition knows what I should do.

·

REFLECTION

I'm learning that my fearful gut reactions are often based on conditioning and are not the voice of my true spirit.

I'm mourning so much more than the loss of the physical presence of the person who died

Yes, of course I'm sad that I can no longer see, touch, and talk with the person who died. But I'm finding that I've lost so much more.

I've lost parts of myself. I may have lost a sense of security and stability in my life. I've lost essential pieces of my future, and I've lost the capacity to feel carefree and maybe experience joy.

This loss has changed so many aspects of my life, and I must acknowledge and mourn all of them.

•

REFLECTION

I must not only mourn the death but also the ripple effect of losses that I am encountering.

The sun will come up tomorrow

Little Orphan Annie sang out this optimistic reminder.
The trouble is, it's often used to encourage people to
suppress or deny the pain of their grief. The message
tends to be: Just tough it out for now, and soon you'll
wake up and everything will be OK.

Actually, I need to embrace today's pain, and tomorrow
I'll need to embrace tomorrow's pain.

Even so, the fact that the sun will indeed
come up tomorrow can give me hope for a new day.
I journey through grief one day at a time, and the
days are different. Just because today was really
hard doesn't necessarily mean tomorrow will be.
I can reset my intention with each new day,
and each day I set forth again anew.

•

REFLECTION
The more I deepen my capacity to be present each day,
the richer each new day becomes.

I'm learning the power of ritual to help me heal

When everyday words and motions are inadequate, I can turn to ritual to help myself heal.

Grief rituals that combine intentionality, actions, symbolism, sequence, presence, heart, and spirit give my grief divine momentum and supercharge my healing.

Grief rituals can be formal group ceremonies such as funerals or memorial services.
They can also be brief, informal, and simple everyday rituals that I enact on my own.

•

REFLECTION

I can make rituals of both celebration and mourning part of my everyday routine.

Embracing my pain is fatiguing

Feeling the normal and necessary pain of my loss is fatiguing work. It tires out my body, my heart, my mind, and my spirit. This is called the "lethargy of grief."

So I need to take breaks from my pain. I also need extra rest.

I might need more sleep than usual, or I might just need to lay my body down several times a day. If my energy is low for a while, that's OK. As long as I'm taking good care of myself, I can trust that my natural energy will eventually return.

·

REFLECTION

My grief slows me down and requires me to rest and renew.

Life isn't either or—it's both/and

Our culture tends to promote the myth that it's our right to be happy. The media inundates us with images of smiling, beautiful people. Happy is supposed to be our baseline, and if we're sad, we've somehow fallen below that baseline (shame on us!) and need to climb back up to it as soon as we can.

But that's not how life works! A true graph of our daily moods and experiences would look more like a movie lie detector test—constant ups and downs. How many different emotions have I felt, at least momentarily, just in the past twenty-four hours? Grateful? Irritated? Bored? Energized? Tense? Sorrowful? Loving? Lethargic?

Life isn't either happy or sad. Every day, it's both happy and sad—and lots and lots of other feelings. And all of it belongs.

•

REFLECTION

I am here for all of it.

Time helps

People say that time heals all wounds,
but that's a grievous misconception. Time alone
does not heal all wounds. Actively befriending and
expressing grief is the best healer.

But *in addition to* intentional mourning, the passage
of time also helps. Grief naturally softens over the
course of years. It never goes away, because its
conjoined twin, love, never goes away, but it becomes
less painful and pronounced.

As I actively dose myself with mourning, day by day,
week by week, I know that I also have time on my
side. It's acting in the background like a river over
rocks, smoothing the sharp edges and carrying me
through the rapids to a safer, more placid place.

·

REFLECTION

I live in the now while maintaining awareness that an
entirely new now is just around the corner.

I don't need approval

Sometimes in my life and in my grief, I seek the approval of others. I want them to think well of me. I hope that they believe I'm a good person and that I'm succeeding—or at least holding my own.

But I don't need to pretend I'm anything other than what I am. So many of the characteristics we tend to think of as worthy can actually be undesirable. For example, "strong" people are often not in touch with their true emotions. "Successful" people are often overly focused on wealth and public image.

I will be what I am. In being vulnerable and open, I'll be sharing the truth of my grief and my life. And my behavior will be congruent with my inner reality.

●

REFLECTION

I approve of myself, no matter how imperfect I may be.

I have a responsibility to truly live

Paradoxically, it is in opening to my broken heart that I open myself to fully living until I die.

I'm on this earth only for a short while. I have the privilege and responsibility to live it fully.

I am responsible to myself, to my maker, and to the person I lost. What if the person who died could see what I'm doing with the remainder of my one precious life? Would they be proud of me? Would they believe that their life and death brought meaning and purpose to mine? I choose to live in ways that the answer to these questions is yes.

•

REFLECTION
I say yes to life in each moment.

I'm blessed by grace

Grace is the divine mechanism by which anything good I've received in life has been given to me.

Grace gave me life. Grace gave me love. Grace generously bestowed on me every gift I've ever been given. After all, I didn't *earn* life. And I haven't always deserved the love I've received.

Cultivating gratitude for this grace, for this life, is key to living forward with joy and meaning.

•

REFLECTION

I am grateful for the grace in every moment.

I devote myself to my broken heart

My broken heart is the most tender, precious thing in all the world.

So I'm gentle with it. I'm kind to it.

I listen to its whispers. I act on its passions. I carry out its yearnings. And I heed its wisdom.

I'm patching my heart together to make it whole again.

·

REFLECTION
With every new patch,
my broken heart grows wiser.

I will not allow myself to die while I'm alive

I've noticed that a lot of living dead walk among us. Some of these people have been defeated by life's many challenges. Some have chosen not to take chances. Some have persuaded themselves that a safe, dreary life is good enough.

I understand that life is hard. I've experienced great loss myself. But I choose to continue to live! I still have promises to keep, people to love, and places to go. I have meaning and purpose to pursue until my dying day.

I choose life.

•

REFLECTION

With every breath, I feel the wonder of life.

I can wallow in my pain

Sometimes I need to wallow in my pain. Wallowing in my sorrow—especially during early grief but also now and then in the months and years to come—isn't bad for me.

Because our culture is grief-avoidant, my wallowing can make others uncomfortable. But wallowing can be constructive. Sometimes I need to withdraw and befriend my pain. Sometimes I need to wallow as a way of refreshing and renewing myself.

Self-empathy and appropriate self-pity are forms of self-preservation and self-care.

·

REFLECTION
I allow myself to feel what I feel.

I embrace mystical experiences

I understand that humans don't know everything there is to know about the mysteries of the universe. Even if I'm a logical, black-and-white kind of thinker, I can still be open to new experiences and unexplainable phenomena.

If I see, hear, or feel the presence of someone who has died, or if I think they might be communicating with me in some way, I'm not going crazy. It might be my mind and heart searching and yearning for the person I love. Or somehow, some way, it might really be happening. Either way, I can choose to accept such experiences and allow them to help me in my grief journey.

·

REFLECTION
I will remember that mystery is something
to be pondered, not explained.

I've been robbed

People sometimes use the old-fashioned word "bereaved" when they're talking about grief. The word bereaved comes from the Old English for "deprive." I've been deprived of the presence of the person I love.

But the origin of the term also connotes something being taken away by force. It's not just that the person I love simply vanished from my life. They were forcibly stolen from me. I was robbed of them.

I don't just feel deprived, I feel robbed. This death is a violation—of the way things were, of companionship, of my sense of security, of my future, and more. As I actively work on the six needs of mourning, I need to express any feelings of deprivation, violation, or injustice I might feel.

•

REFLECTION
To be bereaved is to be "torn apart." So, I may feel deprived and robbed.

I visualize what I desire

My grief naturally has me thinking about my fears and sorrows. I worry about what the future holds. I picture worst-case scenarios.

It's normal for me to explore my fears. But as I continue the journey, I can also choose to explore my desires. What do I want out of the precious life I have left? What do I wish and hope for? What joys and miracles may yet be before me?

When visualizing my fears is causing me to despair, I can consciously choose to shift into visualizing my desires instead. I can picture what I would like to happen in the coming days, weeks, and years. This intentional visualization practice will help me build hope for my future.

•

REFLECTION
I visualize peace, love, and joy.

Grieving is believing

Now that I've come to grief, I better
understand what heartbreaking loss truly feels
like. This loss has me reeling. Other life losses I've
experienced may have felt less devastating.

I'm now a member of a club
I never wanted to join.

When I've witnessed others grieving in the past,
I didn't always fully appreciate what they were
going through. Now I know better. Grieving is
believing. I'll carry my new understanding
into the world with me and use it to support
others with deeper empathy.

●

REFLECTION
The more I see and experience in this world,
the more I realize that I don't have all the answers
and that others have a lot to teach me.

I can live without you

I love you so much, and you died.
You didn't leave me because you *wanted* to leave me…
but you left me nonetheless. And I thought
I couldn't live without you.

Yet here I am, living without you. I hate it, and I wish
it weren't so. But I'm also learning that I don't hate
every minute of it. I still have connections with other
beloved people. I still have passions and joys, hopes
and dreams.

I *can* live without you. And since I'm here
for an unknown number of days or years to come, I
know I should live out those days or
years as fully as I can. So here I go.
I hope I'm making you proud.

•

REFLECTION
My heart beats, and I am grateful.

I start each day with a meditation or prayer

Because I'm getting better at putting meaning and purpose at the center of my life, I'm learning to start each day off right, with a meditation or prayer.

When I wake up, I remind myself that I have choices about how I will move through the day. I can choose to consciously set my intention for the day with an affirmation. I can choose to express gratitude through prayer. I can choose to meditate on a mantra that helps me center and act with loving kindness.

I use affirmations, meditation, and prayer to enhance my quality of life.

·

REFLECTION

I turn to meditation and prayer several times a day, especially whenever I become aware I'm slipping into stress.

Is there life after death?

Since I've come to grief, I've been thinking about
this a lot, and now and then other people want to
talk to me about it as well.

I have my beliefs, and those beliefs might be
shifting or developing new texture these days.
I can consider what others believe—or not.
It's up to me.

But whether or not I believe in the afterlife, what
about for me? Is there life for me after this death?
Yes! I want to continue to live and love deeply
for all the rest of my days. I'm doing the work of
active mourning because I believe that there is life
for me after this death.

•

REFLECTION

As I explore my beliefs, I commit myself
to live fully until I die.

I don't judge people who can't support me

Since our culture doesn't teach people
how to be present to others in grief, I can't expect
everyone in my inner circle of friends and family to be
good grief supporters.

Some people have abandoned me, and others are
giving me terrible advice. They're ignoring me and
even trying to shut me down or shame me for my
normal and necessary grief.

But it's not really their fault. They're behaving as
they were taught to behave. And they have their own
griefs and crises, too. I'm working on having grace for
everyone. I'm not perfect either.

·

REFLECTION

I don't judge. Instead, I remember that people
are doing the best they know to do.

Parts of me died when my loved one died

When my loved one died, I lost their physical presence in my life. I also lost parts of myself.

My relationship with the person who died was an important part of who I was. Now who am I? Plus, I used to have certain beliefs, pastimes, and ways of being in the world, and now I'm forced to rethink some of those.

It feels like a big chunk of myself and my heart died that day, too. I'm grieving that as well. At the same time, I'm working on developing a new self-identity and searching for meaning. I trust that new connections, beliefs, pastimes, and ways of being in the world will eventually coalesce to help patch the hole.

•

REFLECTION

I intend to live this day with meaning and purpose.

I look for the good in myself

I can be hard on myself in grief. I sometimes think I'm not doing well enough, not trying hard enough, not making any progress.

When I catch myself thinking this way, it's a sign that I need to be more self-compassionate. As long as I'm befriending and expressing my grief, I'm doing just fine. There's no timetable and no yardstick.

I choose to look for the good in my days, my life, and myself. Even as I'm being present to my pain, I intentionally honor my best qualities and my strengths. Looking for the good in myself helps me rebuild my self-identity and find new meaning and purpose.

•

REFLECTION
I look for the good and shared humanity in everyone.

I'm finding a balance between being helped by others and helping myself

I absolutely need and deserve the support of others during my time of grief. But in an effort to help me, some people in my life may try to rescue me.
They might breach my boundaries and move to take over too much of my life.

I'm learning to reach out for and accept help while at the same time doing for myself what I *want* to do for myself. Sometimes I may need a lot of help, and sometimes I may need just a little.

·

REFLECTION
It's good to be vulnerable, and it's good to reestablish independence. It's a question of balance.

I look for role models

Some people seem to live their grief with grace. They suffer and authentically express their suffering, but they also keep living and loving and helping and doing.

I look for role models in grief. I might find them in books, on TV, or in my own life. Whenever I see someone who has suffered great loss not only surviving but thriving, I can look to them for mentorship.

I can always learn and grow.
Grief role models can help me.

•

REFLECTION
I naturally gravitate toward people who
are authentic role models.

The life of the person I love mattered

When a person dies and vanishes from this world, they not only leave behind a physical, empty hole in the present—they also leave behind a void of meaning.

This person lived and died—and now they're gone. Did their life amount to something? Did it matter? Will they be remembered?

Here's what I know: Yes! Their life mattered! They mattered to me, and they mattered to others. They even mattered in ways I wasn't a part of and know nothing about. I'm working on finding ways to memorialize and honor the life and death of this one precious life.

•

REFLECTION

The life of every butterfly impacts the entire world.

I'm the expert of my own grief

Grief is a common experience, and people who are grieving have many thoughts and feelings in common.

But still, my grief is unique. My life story is unique. My personality is unique. The relationship I had with the person who died was unique. Like my love for the person who died, my grief is a one-of-a-kind miracle.

While it's important to talk to others about my grief, only I can decide if their advice makes sense for me. And only I can decide how to apply the ten touchstones to my experience.

•

REFLECTION

I'm open to learning and growth, yet I'm also strong in self-understanding and firmly rooted in my core values.

I speak kindly to everyone— including myself

One thing my grief journey is teaching me is the importance of kindness.

When others are kind to me, even in tiny ways, it makes such an enormous difference. I feel seen and supported by their kindness. And when I'm kind to myself, I feel comforted and safe.

So as I venture out into the world, I'm remembering to speak kindly to everyone I come in contact with. I speak kindly not only to my friends and family but also to coworkers, neighbors, store clerks, service people, and strangers. I also speak kindly to myself. My self-talk is becoming more and more gentle, supportive, and positive.

·

REFLECTION
Kindness is the way.

Death is a normal part of life

As I become more comfortable thinking and talking about my loss and grief, I also become more comfortable thinking and talking about death.

Death is just as much a part of human life as any other facet of existence. It's normal, and it's even necessary because without death, our planet couldn't survive.

I'm befriending grief, but I'm also learning to befriend death. And in befriending death, I'm getting better at offering my empathetic presence to others in all kinds of life circumstances. I'm no longer closing my eyes and my heart to the end of life, even my own.

•

REFLECTION

The hole in my life created by the death of someone I love is so hard to reconcile myself to, but death itself I understand and befriend.

Certain days are harder

Holidays, anniversaries, birthdays, and other special days are often more painful in grief.

On these days, it's normal for me to especially miss the person who died. I want them present. I yearn to have them here with me.

On these days, I need to be extra gentle with myself. I will not overextend myself, and I will allow time for rest, grief, and mourning.

•

REFLECTION

On special days, I integrate remembering the person who died into the celebrations. Mourning and celebrating are both rich in love and belong together.

Struggling does not mean failing

It's normal to struggle in grief. Grief is hard!
Actually, it's the hardest thing there is!

So of course I'm struggling. I'm embracing
and expressing my grief, but sometimes it
feels like I'm trying to tame a wild horse.
I get thrown and kicked around.

But struggling isn't the same as failing.
The only failures in grief are denying its necessity
or keeping it all inside. Struggling means
I'm doing the work.

•

REFLECTION

I trust the work of mourning to get
me where I want to go.

I'm all about me right now

If my grief is making me focus more on myself
and less on others right now, that's normal.
My grief needs me. It needs my attention and
understanding. It needs me to spend time
acknowledging it and expressing it.

When I spend this time on me, I'm not being
selfish. I'm carrying out essential self-care.

Only through the necessary work of active
mourning and self-care will I be able to return to
effectively supporting others.

·

REFLECTION
Grief naturally turns me inward,
but that doesn't mean I'm being selfish.

I'm aware of the strengths and weaknesses of my support system

I need other people to help me in my grief.
I deserve empathy, caring, and encouragement.
I must also be willing and able to
accept this support.

My natural need for ongoing support has made
the strengths and weaknesses of my support
system apparent. Where there are weaknesses,
I must be proactive about finding ways
to fill the gaps.

·

REFLECTION
I'm meaningfully connected with others
in my life, and I am an essential
connection in the lives of others.

I'm doing my best

As long as I'm befriending and mourning my grief in doses, I can trust that I'm doing my best.

Life's not perfect. I'm not perfect.
Other people in my life aren't perfect.
We're all doing the best we can.

I aspire to be grief-aware, authentic, and kind.

·

REFLECTION
I am where I am in my grief journey.
I acknowledge I'm doing the best that I can.

I've decided to live again

After a significant life loss, we all naturally
get pulled under by grief. We descend first,
sinking down and under. Grief gets
harder before it gets easier.

After a time, we touch bottom. We inhabit the
deepest depths of our despair. And then what?

And then we have a choice. Do we choose to
ascend or to stay there? We can die while we are
alive, or we can intentionally choose to find our
way back to truly living again. As for me, I've
decided I want to live again.

·

REFLECTION
Life is a privilege, and choosing to live
and love it fully honors that privilege as
well as the person who died.

I appreciate me

What a wonderful thing it is to be a unique human being here on earth. What an amazing privilege it is to be me.

My life isn't perfect. I'm not perfect. I'm not grieving and mourning perfectly. So what?! Perfection is only an illusion, anyway. Plus, idiosyncrasies are more interesting.

I appreciate the person who died and the relationship we shared. I appreciate my friends and family. And I appreciate me. Each of us is worthy of acknowledgment, respect, and celebration.

•

REFLECTION
I appreciate every aspect of myself, even the challenging parts.

I'm not giving myself a timetable for healing

When I feel like my healing is taking too long—
or that I'm going backward instead of forward—
I might lose confidence in my capacity to heal.
I might lose hope that my life will ever get better.

So if I'm ever feeling stuck or hopeless,
I'll remember to take stock of any timetable
expectations—conscious or subconscious—
I might have for healing. There's no "correct"
duration of time to deeply grieve.
There's no schedule. There's no right or
wrong sequence of "stages."

·

REFLECTION
There are no rewards for speed.
It will take as long as it takes.

The dark night of the soul is dark indeed

When my loved one died, I was plunged into the darkness. My pain was all-consuming, and the loss felt unsurvivable.

I experienced what some philosophers have called the dark night of the soul. It's awful and scary. It hurts *so much*. And it took much longer than a night. It lasted weeks and months. For some people the profoundest pain goes on for years.

Yet I learned that if I allowed myself to sit still in the blackness without trying to fight it, deny it, or run away from it, it had something to teach me. The very moment that I began to befriend the darkness became the moment that I began, ever so slowly, to move toward the light.

•

REFLECTION

I have nothing to fear from the dark.

I can retreat to my comfort zone

In grief, my comfort zone is the place and the activity that I find comforting. When I'm fatigued and worn down, I know I can retreat to my comfort zone for rest and renewal.

I might cozy up on the couch and binge my favorite TV show. Or I might putter around in my yard. Or I might shoot hoops in the driveway.

Whatever and wherever helps me relax and feel that sense of comfort and relief—that's my comfort zone. It's a good place to be.

●

REFLECTION

Through mindfulness, I can find comfort wherever I am.

I wasn't ready

I wasn't ready for this death. Even if it was expected, I still wasn't really ready.

The finality of death always comes as a shock. There's no preparing for it. There's no magic grief preventive.

I dislike feeling blindsided. I hate having the rug pulled out from under me. But that's what happened. And now I'm working on mustering the courage to surrender to the reality. Resistance to what is only causes me more suffering.

•

REFLECTION
As hard as it is, I'm working to acknowledge the reality of this death.

I invest in important relationships

The people I love play an important role
in my wellbeing.

Connected relationships with my family and
friends can motivate me to take care of myself—to
eat right, exercise, and get regular medical care.
My family and friends can be an important buffer
from the stresses of everyday life.

The important relationships in my life need
tending. I have to spend time with the people I
love, and I have to offer them focused presence,
empathy, and care. In doing so, I'm likely to
receive the same in return.

·

REFLECTION
Strong relationships are central to my life.

I am present to whatever presents itself

When I am present in this moment, I'm open to experiencing whatever arises in this moment.

Grief thoughts and feelings can come up at any time. When they do, that means that they're trying to get my attention. In fact, they need my awareness and attention so they can be experienced and moved through.

Whenever possible, I give attention to my grief in the moment that it arises. The more present and responsive I am to my grief, the more readily it becomes an integral part of me and my continuing life.

·

REFLECTION
When I attend to my grief,
I bring living back into my life.

I'm a student of life

One of the main things I'm learning from my grief is that I still have a lot to learn.

Before my loss, I thought I knew a thing or two. I was more confident about my life. But this death has shaken me to my core. It's making me question all kinds of assumptions, decisions, and beliefs.

So now I'm approaching life with a learner's heart. I'm curious instead of overconfident. I'm open instead of closed. I'm flexible instead of fixed.

·

REFLECTION

Every day I experience and I learn.

Overthinking compounds my grief

My grieving mind is difficult to turn off. Its chaotic chatter and questioning cause me anxiety and unease. It constantly wants to think about my to-do list, my fears, my regrets, my "what-ifs," and more.

But I find that if I can calm my mind, I become less tense and my grief relaxes. Breathing exercises, meditation, prayer, journaling, and complete immersion in activities I enjoy are all techniques I can employ to tame my mind.

Besides, healing grief is mostly a spiritual journey— not a cognitive one. I can't think my way through my grief. I have to feel it and be with it in the now.

•

REFLECTION

I observe my thoughts as they float past me.

Right now, there's no loss harder than mine

Comparing the relative difficulty of people's losses is a zero-sum game. It's not that helpful to think about whether my loss is easier or harder than someone else's.

But since grief is an internal experience, all I can ever fully experience is my own loss. I can definitely empathize with the losses of others, and I can imagine what they might feel like to me, but I only completely inhabit my loss.

So to me, my loss is the hardest, even if it's the kind of loss that our culture considers expected or lesser (such as the death of an elderly person or a beloved pet). I'm treating my grief and mourning as fully justified and legitimate—because it is.

·

REFLECTION
I consciously choose not to compare losses.

I am both darkness and light

In Greek mythology, Persephone became queen of the underworld. Living happily on earth with her family, she was kidnapped by Hades, and after some trickery and back-and-forth, was forced to remain there with him six months of every year. From then on, Persephone embodied the dualities of winter/summer, evil/good, and darkness/light.

All of us are Persephones, really. The trick is in awakening to the reality that the dark periods in our lives are not shameful, wrong, or bad. They are as normal and natural as any other aspect of human life.

·

REFLECTION
I embrace my whole self.

Remembering the past makes hoping for the future possible

I know that remembering the person who
died and the time we spent together is part
of my healing process.

I actively work at remembering by talking about my
memories as well as embracing stories about the
person who died that other people share with me.
I display photos of the person who died, and I might
have some special keepsakes that help me remember.
I don't shy away from visiting places that
hold memories. I also go through photo
albums and watch videos.

If I have unpleasant memories,
I talk about those, too, and I see a counselor
if I need to process traumatic memories.

●

My past is an integral part of my now.

My personality determines, in part, my grief and mourning

My personality was shaped in my childhood. Whether I'm an introvert or an extrovert, a thinker or a doer, a silly or serious person, I am who I am. And how I naturally grieve and mourn is an expression, in part, of my personality.

I have the right to grieve and mourn in ways that feel right for me. Still, I should be on the watch for tendencies and habits that don't serve me well in grief. For example, if I'm not comfortable expressing my emotions, now is the time for me to work on emotional intelligence and the capacity to share feelings outside myself.

•

REFLECTION

My unique and one-of-a-kind personality will continue to influence my grief and mourning.

It's not me—it's my ego

When I'm feeling apart from others in some way—maybe I feel inferior or superior or wronged or competitive or lacking or judgmental—I realize it's not me talking, it's my ego.

My ego thinks I'm separate and different from everyone else, and it tries to build me (and just me) up. But my spirit knows that I'm deeply connected to everyone else and that we are all fundamentally one.

I can use my grief journey to become more aware of my ego and dissolve it. My true essence is loving, kind, accepting, and generous. And it's in those qualities that I will find my ongoing meaning and purpose.

·

REFLECTION

The more I let go of ego, the richer my life becomes.

I'm proud of my grief

Our culture implies that grief is weak and shameful, but there is nothing further from the truth.

My deep grief is proof that I have deeply loved. And that love is my proudest accomplishment. I don't make grief my identity, but I definitely honor it.

And so I mourn openly and authentically. I don't hide my grief but instead wear it on my sleeve. "Yes, I'm someone who prioritizes love!" I say. "My heart has been cracked wide open. I am devastated but at the same time also proud to have the privilege of counting myself among those who have loved well enough to become brokenhearted."

•

REFLECTION

There is no greater gift in life than love.

As I'm picking up the pieces, I get to choose which pieces to pick up

Great loss is like a reset button. It started my life over.

Now that I'm in my new life, I'm working on creating my new normal. I'm looking at all the pieces of my old life scattered around me. And I'm stooping to pick them up.

But wait! Maybe I don't want to pick all of them up. Maybe there are some pieces that no longer serve me. Maybe there are some that weren't working well for me even before the loss. I don't have to reconstitute my life using *all* the old pieces. If I want, I can choose to leave some of them behind.

●

REFLECTION

I will pick some things up: I will lay some things down.

I can't do everything

When I expect too much of myself, my grief can become overwhelming.

Whatever I can do today is enough.
There is always tomorrow
(and if there's not, that's OK, too).

My choices are limitless, but my time here on earth is not. As long as I am present to my love, my grief, and my life each day, I am doing what I can. In fact, through conscious presence I am actually doing much more than I do on days when I am mindlessly doing too much.

·

REFLECTION
I am here to be, not do.

I need to rethink and retell the story

I think about the death a lot. I find myself replaying what happened during the time periods before, during, and after the death and wondering about moments I wasn't there for.

I need to talk about what happened, too. I may need to say the same things over and over again and ask questions aloud.

Rethinking and retelling the story in these ways helps bring my head and heart together. It helps me make sense of what happened and eventually find some peace with it.

•

REFLECTION

There is awesome power in retelling my story.

I'm responsible for my intentions and my responses

It would be great if I had the power to control what happens in my life and in the lives of those I care about—but of course, I don't. This loss has made me feel my lack of control even more deeply.

What I do have control over are my intentions and my responses. I can set my intentions for what I plan to do and how I plan to be. And I can decide how I will act in any given moment.

If I mourn intentionally and I respond mindfully, I will know that I'm taking responsibility for my healing.

●

REFLECTION

I can be self-responsible without taking myself too seriously.

I am not "over it" and never will be

Despite what some people think, I won't "get over" my grief. I will always grieve this loss.

My grief is part of my love. How could I ever relinquish that love? Why would I ever want to?

Instead of "getting over it," I'm learning to integrate my grief into my ongoing life. Through active mourning, I'm putting my arms around it and welcoming it into my life. It's not a temporary visitor—it is a new, albeit difficult, part of who I am. The more I work to integrate it, the more at home it will become.

•

REFLECTION

My grief is a bittersweet presence in my life.
It's an inextricable part of my forever-love
for the person who died.

When I'm in distress, I destress

All of my thoughts and feelings in grief are normal.
They're also necessary. How do I know they're
necessary? If I'm having them, that means that in that
moment, at least, they're necessary for me. So I'm
learning to be with my thoughts and feelings and to
express them no matter what they are.

But sometimes I get really distressed. I can be so down
or upset that I feel like I can't survive. That's when I
know it's time to destress. I open my stress-management
toolkit and select a practice or activity that helps me feel
calmer and more even-keeled.

Befriending and mourning my grief authentically don't
mean living in a constant state of distress. Instead, they
mean encountering my grief in doses, taking extra care
or seeking extra help when I'm distressed, and giving
myself lots of pampering and respite in between.

·

REFLECTION
I give attention to my distress by
practicing good self-care.

I wish I'd been a better person

I'm not perfect. I have regrets. When I think about the person who died, I wish I'd done some things differently in our relationship and in the time I had with them.

My regretful feelings are normal and natural, and exploring and expressing them is part of my grief journey. But the second phase is learning from them. In what ways will I change my life based on the hard lessons I've learned?

The good news is that I still have time to be that better person! Working to do things differently in my life moving forward is part of how I honor the person who died.

•

REFLECTION

As I awaken to who I really am, I live out my days with more awareness, compassion, and kindness.

Faith isn't the absence of fear—it's trusting to go forward despite the fear

During my grief journey, I've been afraid of lots of things—the prospect of life without the person who died, for one.

Some degree of worry and anxiety in grief are normal, but even when I'm afraid, I can still go on. As long as I'm actively mourning, I can choose to have faith that I'm moving in the direction of less pain and more joy.

I don't know what life will bring, but I have faith that in the mix there will be peace, goodness, and joy.

·

REFLECTION

Fear shuts me down. Faith opens me up.

Problems are actually opportunities

Life is change, and some change feels bad. That's where my grief comes from.

But what if I think of those bad-feeling changes not as problems to be solved or resolved but instead as opportunities to be ventured?

My grief isn't a problem. It's the natural and necessary sequel to my love during a time of change. But this time of change is also replete with opportunity. I'm learning to see the concepts of "problems" and "opportunities" anew.

·

REFLECTION

The more I think in terms of opportunities instead of problems, the richer and deeper my experience of life becomes.

I imagine the great beyond

Whether I'm someone who believes in an afterlife or not, it's normal to wonder what happens after death and what might exist beyond our own limited capacities to understand.

The universe is a fathomless place. Scientists now estimate there are two trillion galaxies. By far, there is a lot more we don't know than we do know.

When I imagine the great beyond, I might think about the person who died or God or alternate universes or quantum physics or my hopes and dreams. Such imaginings help remind me to relinquish the illusion of control and just enjoy the ride.

•

REFLECTION

I marvel at the privilege of getting to be a human on this earth, if only for a blink of time.

My acceptance changes and deepens

Over time, I'm finding that my acceptance of the death is changing. It's getting deeper and more nuanced.

At first it was hard to even believe, let alone accept. I kept expecting the person who died to walk through the door. But over time I began to accept the death in a factual way. Yes, this precious body is no longer animated by life here on earth.

Later, I found myself accepting the death more as a presence in my life. The fact of the death is a given that happened in the past. But now the emotional and spiritual reality of the death lives beside me each and every day, and I am still finding new ways of integrating it.

•

REFLECTION

I will continue to work toward accepting the death and freeing myself to live until I die.

I'm part of the slow grief movement

The slow grief movement seeks to overturn the dominant cultural misconception that we should hurry up and get over our grief.

Grief takes as long as it takes. There are no rewards for speed.

I experience slow grief, and I bear witness to slow grief in others. We companion each other on this naturally glacial, difficult journey.

·

REFLECTION
A life lived slowly and on purpose is a life well lived.

I yearn for the person who died

I miss the person who died. Actually,
I *yearn for* the person who died. I feel an
ache of longing that doesn't subside.

I want them here with me!

As I learn to establish a new kind of relationship
with the person who died—one of memory
instead of presence, and perhaps one based on my
potential belief that our separation is temporary—
the ache of my yearning will slowly transform into
a new way of loving the precious person I miss.

·

REFLECTION

As I mourn, I allow myself to shift the
relationship from presence to memory.

I'm grieving my future

I miss the person who died. I'm grieving
the loss of their physical presence in
my life right here, right now.

But I'm also grieving the future I'd imagined
and hoped for. The person who died was part
of that future. I'm forced to give up certain
assumptions and dreams.

I'll be creating a different future, but it will
take a while for me to settle into. In the meantime,
I'm allowing myself to feel and live with and
express the loss of the path I had intended to
travel but cannot.

·

REFLECTION

As much as possible, I live for today and try to not to
set too many expectations for the future.

I honor my pain

I can't go around the wilderness of my grief.
Instead, I must journey through it.

My pain is part of my life. I honor my pain by
acknowledging it, valuing it, spending time with
it, and listening to what it has to teach me.

The capacity to love requires the necessity to
mourn. I honor my pain in doses.

•

REFLECTION

Life is change, and I flow with change.
I open my arms to joy, pain, and all life experiences.

It's possible for me to thrive again

I'm working on surviving. I'm actively mourning to give myself momentum on the healing journey so I can work through my necessary grief.

Eventually, it's my intention to reconcile my grief. In reconciliation, my grief will be fully integrated into my ongoing life. It will always be an integral, inextricable part of who I am, but it will no longer be my main preoccupation.

As I move toward reconciliation, I can make choices that steer me toward living my ongoing life with increasing meaning. I can thrive again. Thriving isn't about outward measures of success. It's about experiencing inner purpose, gratitude, and connection.

·

REFLECTION

After I survive, I will commit myself to thrive.

Grief work is soul work

Nourishing my grieving soul is a matter of
surrendering to the mystery of grief.

I also nourish my soul by devoting time and
attention to whatever gives my life richness and
purpose. By trying to develop my potentials.
By striving to give back. By having and
expressing gratitude. By helping others.
By living my life on purpose.

I work to nourish my transforming soul.

•

Circumstances come and go, but my soul is forever.

I want to make the most of the rest of my life

This death has really made it clear to me that life is short. The person who died may not have been given all the time and opportunity they needed to do what they wanted to do.

But here I am. I'm still here. And I get to choose how I look at the remainder of my days, no matter how many there might be.

I choose to make the most of the rest of my life. During my time of grief, that means actively embracing my grief and mourning in doses. It also means strengthening connections with others I care about and working on rebuilding my self-identity in the ways I find most meaningful.

·

REFLECTION

Here I am. I might as well make the most of it.

I sit in the wound of my grief

Experiencing the necessary sadness of grief is sometimes called "sitting in your wound."

When I sit in the wound of my grief, I surrender to it. I acquiesce to the instinct to slow down and turn inward. I allow myself to appropriately wallow in the pain. I shut the world out for a time so that, eventually, I've created space to let the world back in.

Sitting in the wound of my grief teaches me that I'm strong enough to withstand it. I have the capacity to meet and embrace the depths of my grief. And when I realize this, my grief becomes ever-so-slightly less overwhelming.

•

REFLECTION

I bear compassionate witness to all of my feelings.

I'm a grief explorer

I'm an explorer of this wilderness of my grief.
I don't have a map. The only compass I have is the
six needs of mourning and the ten touchstones—
and they're just rough guides, not turn-by-turn
Google Maps instructions.

So I embark, I roam, and I discover. I encounter
strange and challenging features. I see what there
is to see. I get lost sometimes.

I'm here to experience it all.

•

REFLECTION
Exploring life is why I'm here.

Sometimes my grief scares me

Some days my grief is so terrible and powerful that it scares me. It might make me act out in aggressive ways. Or it sends me into the depths of despair, rendering me unable to think or move.

On those days, all I can do is hold on and ride out the storm. As with any storm, the wildness is temporary. In minutes or hours, I'll feel more settled again, and equilibrium will be restored.

I can also reach out to a friend when my grief is especially scary. They can help me weather the storm.

·

REFLECTION

I experience strong feelings with self-compassion.

And I lived meaningfully ever after

That's what I hope people will say about me when I die. They will tell the story of how I suffered great loss, but I met it openly and authentically. I befriended it. I learned from it. And it made me a more empathetic person who reveled in relationships and what really matters in life.

I don't get to live happily ever after. Not one-hundred-percent happily. Pretty much no one does.

But I can live meaningfully ever after. And that is what I intend to do.

●

REFLECTION

I am aware of the meaning in each moment.

I'm working on mindfulness

My grief often takes me to memories of the past and worries about the future. These are normal parts of my grief. But when I find myself living in the past and projecting the unknown future too much—at the expense of missing my life— I remember to work on mindfulness.

Mindfulness reminds me that I'm alive right here, right now. I take in everything my five senses can detect in the moment. I pay attention to my breath. I am present to the people who are here with me.

These practices help me learn how to live again.

·

REFLECTION
This moment is where I live.

I can evade my grief when I need to

I befriend my grief by encountering and expressing it in small doses.

But sometimes a wave of grief may come over me at a time when I'm not able to welcome it. I might be working or interacting with another person or busy with an essential task. When this happens, I can choose to evade or postpone my grief for a short while.

I can promise my grief that I'll meet it at a later time that same day or very soon. If I cry or lose emotional control for a minute, it's OK. That's totally normal and understandable. But it's also OK to use techniques to re-center or distract myself so I can continue functioning for the time being.

•

REFLECTION

By attending to my five senses and my breathing, I can center myself in only what is necessary of me in this moment.

I choose stabilizing thoughts

Grief is naturally chaotic and stressful. When I need a break from the chaos and stress, I meditate on a thought or image that stabilizes me.

First, I find a thought that makes me feel peaceful or good. It can be anything. It might be something like, "I am thankful for this day" or "My soul is peaceful" or "I place my trust in God." I repeat this mantra to myself, silently or aloud, while breathing slowly and deeply. I may also gaze on a calming image of my choice while I speak the affirmation. I continue to do this until I feel calm and present.

This intentional practice of stabilizing my thoughts and mood is something I get better at the more I do it.

·

REFLECTION

I know that all destabilizing thoughts are mostly the product of my ego and fear.

Each day I make it a priority to do something that gives me pleasure

I need something to look forward to,
especially when I'm immersed in the pain of grief.
That's why I plan ahead for pleasure breaks.

What can I add to my calendar for tomorrow
that I know will help me feel at least a smidgen of
hope, happiness, or relief, if only for an hour or so?
I ask myself this question each night before bed.
It helps me wake up in the morning with
something to look forward to.

I need and deserve enjoyment. If I'm having trouble
experiencing any pleasure at all for a long period
of time, that means I need to talk to a friend or
counselor about my depression.

•

REFLECTION
Despite my grief, I can seek out times of
pleasure and enjoyment.

I feel so disorganized and mixed up

This great loss in my life has me feeling so confused and disorganized. My thoughts and emotions are jumbled and chaotic.
I'm having a hard time with short-term memory. And I can't get anything done!

It is disorienting to feel so scattered.

Disorganization in grief always comes before reorganization, though. My mind is working to integrate this unbelievable new reality. As it does so over time, my capacity to think clearly and accomplish necessary tasks will return to me.

·

REFLECTION

Out of my disorientation will come reorientation.
I must be patient as this naturally unfolds.

I nurture my inner life

My divine spark is the glow of my soul within me. It's the source of my meaning and purpose.

When I nurture my inner life, I nurture my divine spark. When I carve out time in my days for reflection, daydreaming, imagination, and creation, I'm building my inner spark into a stronger flame.

I am both an outward-facing community member with a meaningful life of connection and an inward-facing individual with a rich inner life. I must nurture both aspects of myself to move toward healing in grief.

·

REFLECTION

Putting my inner life first enables me to act meaningfully in the world.

I seek divine momentum in my grief and mourning

Sometimes when I've actively expressed my grief, I'll notice afterward that I feel hopeful or good about my progress toward reconciliation. I'll realize that I'm learning and, slowly and over time, healing.

These moments of awareness are indicators of "divine momentum." In grief, divine momentum is that experience of being carried along by doing what is helpful and necessary.

Divine momentum is the opposite of being stuck in grief. When I'm feeling stuck—which will happen, too, sometimes—I can remember to turn to those mourning activities and practices that respark my divine momentum.

•

REFLECTION

I live in gratitude as I flow with life.

There is beauty in darkness

Grief is so painful and terrible. Yet it is the truth, and bearing witness to the truth of all human experiences reveals their beauty.

In the song "The Music of the Night," from *The Phantom of the Opera*, the disfigured man, Erik, who lives and hides in the dark caverns below the opera house, extols the beauty and virtues of darkness. He says that darkness sharpens our sensations, stirs our imagination, and invites surrender.

My grief is dark and painful, but I am learning to see the beauty of its authenticity, truth, and love.

•

REFLECTION

I see the beauty in everything that is true and authentic.

Baby steps add up

I'm taking baby steps to journey with intention
through the wilderness of my grief.

Every day, another baby step or two.
And some days, a baby step or two back.
It's slow going, but it does the job.

I've heard it said that a journey of 1,000 miles
begins with a single step. That's grief in a nutshell.

·

REFLECTION

If I concern myself with baby steps, I can trust that
the journey will take care of itself.

Yes, I can be moody

Sometimes my feelings swing wildly from moment to moment or day to day. I don't feel better and better each day. It's difficult to see progress day to day.

Grief twists and turns like a mountainous trail. When I'm having ups and downs and unexpected pain, I'm patient with myself.

I trust that as long as I'm experiencing and expressing my authentic emotions each day, over the long haul my grief will indeed soften.

•

REFLECTION
I recognize mood swings as fleeting.

I choose to live congruently

Congruency is when my inner feelings and values match my behaviors. My grief is helping me become more aware of my inner feelings and values and express them authentically.

For example, if I value peace and kindness, I act with peace and kindness when I encounter other people throughout my day. Or if I care about the environment, I make daily choices that are gentle on the earth.

Congruency feels "right." It helps me know I am living with meaning and purpose.

•

REFLECTION

I strive to be congruent as I express my grief into mourning.

I need other people to help me with my grief

Grief is a solo activity because it happens inside me. But mourning is how I heal, and mourning is not a solo activity. When I share my thoughts and feelings outside of myself, I engage the empathy of others. And their empathy and support help me heal.

Sharing my pain with others doesn't make it go away, but it does make it more bearable. Reaching out for help also connects me to other people and strengthens bonds of love and connection that make life seem worth living again.

●

REFLECTION
I feel well-connected and deeply loved.

I'm sometimes helpless

I wish I had some control over the lives of my loved ones so I could save them from pain, sickness, loss, and death. But I don't. That's not how life works.

When something bad happens to someone I love, I'm helpless to "fix it." And now someone I love has died, and I naturally feel helpless.

Surrendering to my helplessness in this circumstance is part of my grief work. I try to think of ways the outcome could or should have been different. I protest the outcome by getting angry. But ultimately, coming to terms with my helplessness in the face of death is an essential stop on my journey.

•

REFLECTION

I'm not here to control life but rather to experience it.

Please witness my grief, and I'll witness yours

The sixth need of mourning is receiving support from others. Part of this is simply about being seen.

I need my loss acknowledged. I need others to let me know that *they* know that I've suffered a significant life change and I'm hurting. They do this by phoning me, stopping by, bringing a casserole, sending a sympathy card, following up with a text, and just generally connecting. On an ongoing basis, they continue to bear witness to my grief by staying in touch and by listening to me when I need to talk.

I need them, and now I know that they'll need me when they experience a loss. We'll bear witness to each other.

·

REFLECTION

One human bearing kind witness to another is a thing of beauty.

I grieve many aspects of the person who died

I miss so much about the person who died.
I miss knowing they're there. I miss their voice.
I miss their smile. I miss talking with them.
I miss their hands and their eyes and their
memories. I miss their unique personalities.

But maybe I don't miss everything about the
person who died. Perhaps there were harmful,
problematic, or lacking qualities, too.

I grieve the things I miss, and I also grieve the
things I don't miss but wish had been different.

·

REFLECTION
I see value in mourning both what I miss
and what I don't miss.

I say thank you

My grief journey has me working on gratitude. Gratitude is the internal awareness and feeling of being thankful for the gifts in my life.

But to take that idea one step further, I must also express my gratitude. I must say thank you wherever and whenever thanks are due. Thank-yous bring my gratitude full circle and help build a culture of gratitude.

Meister Eckhart was a 14th-century Christian theologian and mystic. He said, "If the only prayer you said was thank you, that would be enough." Who can I thank today?

•

REFLECTION

"I love you" and "thank you" may be the only two responses to another person I truly ever need.

I know that I will survive this

Grief is hard, and grief is painful. Yet nonetheless, I must embrace and express my grief right now. I must do the work of mourning.

Yet even as I grieve and actively mourn, I hold tight to the certainty that my grief will eventually soften. My pain will diminish. It will never completely disappear—because, thank goodness, my love will never disappear—but it will dull, fade, and move into the background of my daily life.

I am surviving. I'm also doing the grief work I need to do so that one day I can thrive again.

·

REFLECTION

No matter what happens today, I know that I'm privileged to love and to be alive.

Trying to hurry up my grief makes it take longer

When I get impatient with my grief and just want it to be over, I find that it stalls.

When I'm patient with my grief, on the other hand, and allow it to take up the time, space, and attention it needs, I find that it has momentum.

Grief isn't a race, and there are no rewards for speed. But the ironic thing is that befriending my feelings and expressing them, day by day, is actually the quickest way through the most challenging time of my grief. It's like the fable of the tortoise and the hare. The best strategy is letting my grief be the tortoise that it is.

•

REFLECTION

The only thing that hurrying things up ever accomplishes is missing out on life.

I talk kindly to myself

In grief, if I'm not careful, my self-talk can discourage me.

When I catch myself judging my own supposed lack of strength, courage, or progress, I make a conscious effort to redirect. I begin to talk to myself more kindly and encouragingly.

"You deserve to be well taken care of," I say. "You have been wounded deeply, and you need TLC from yourself and others. You are good and courageous. You are enough."

.

REFLECTION

Self-compassion is a critical ingredient that allows me to integrate this loss into my life.

I'm learning to befriend uncertainty

Before my loss, I was more certain about my life. The loss has thrown me into a period of doubt and uncertainty.

I don't know what to do. I don't know what will happen next. It's uncomfortable, this uncertainty.

The funny thing is, the old certainty and stability I felt was the true anomaly. Life is actually more change than stasis. So I'm learning that there can be peace and joy in going with the flow.

·

REFLECTION
Uncertainty is the only certainty.

I yearn for touch

After a significant loss, grieving people who are hugged, touched, and visited by friends and family report feeling comforted and supported. I may or may not consider myself a hugger. But even people who didn't think of themselves as huggy, touchy people before a loss may find themselves craving physical proximity and touch after a loss.

When we are touched in comforting ways, our bodies are flooded with dopamine, serotonin, and oxytocin. These feel-good hormones help regulate our mood and make us feel calmer and happier. Lack of touch has the opposite effect.

·

REFLECTION

When I yearn for touch, I seek out appropriate ways to feed my touch starvation.

I am developing a new self-identity

The way I see myself, and perhaps the way the world sees me, has been affected by this death.

My life is different now. Certain life circumstances have changed as a result of the death. I may not have wanted these changes, but I'm working to acknowledge and embrace them nonetheless.

I am creating a new me.

·

REFLECTION

I'm well-served to ask myself, "How am I now different than I was before?"

I set my intention to heal

I am committed to healing my grief. I set my intention to heal by envisioning the future I desire and by being an active participant in my grief. I verbalize my grief intentions out loud to myself and to others.

I am committed to befriending my pain. The alternative is to shut down and deny my pain, which is to die while I am still alive. That is not the future I desire.

Slowly and in doses, I can and will return to life and begin to live again in ways that put stars back into my sky.

•

REFLECTION

I use the power of intention to live well each day and steer toward tomorrow.

I can learn to reframe my thoughts

My grief is normal and natural, but sometimes I get caught up in "dirty-pain," negative thinking. I catastrophize or tell myself stories about how things are only going to get worse. I spiral into obsessive worry or despair.

But I can learn to reframe my thinking. I can learn new thought habits that help me feel better and grow more resilient.

When I catch myself in negative thought patterns, I can meditate on a positive idea instead, such as, "I choose to focus on what I can control," "I choose hope," or "My life is filled with possibility." I can also talk to a friend or see a counselor to help me redirect my anxiety.

·

REFLECTION

Thoughts are often not reality.

My grief is fluid and fickle

My grief changes all the time.
It might feel different today than it will tomorrow.
It might feel different in five minutes
than it does right now.

My grief circles back on itself. It jumps from one
thing to another. It gets snagged now and then on
parts that are especially hard for me.

My grief is a lot of different thoughts and feelings
all at once. And the mixture is
constantly morphing.

That's just how grief works. And it's OK.

·

REFLECTION

I make space for my ever-changing thoughts and
feelings, and I allow them to come and go.

I cannot "think through" my grief

While I'm tempted to want to think about my grief in my head, I must allow it to descend into my heart.

If I insulate myself from feeling by always thinking, I will shut down. I have come to the realization that it is in being open to my feelings that I discover renewed meaning and purpose in my life.

•

REFLECTION

I must allow my grief to go from my head to my heart.

Grief *can* be shared

There's a popular misconception that
says that grief can't be shared—that each grieving
person just has to figure out how to get
through it on their own.

In reality, grief must be shared!
That's what healthy mourning is all about.

While it's true that I experience my own unique
inner grief, my experience has a lot in common
with the grief of others. Plus, we need to support
each other in our grief. We need to talk about it
and normalize it. We need to bear witness to and
companion each other.

Just as we share love, we must share grief.

·

REFLECTION
I am part of the tight-knit web of humanity.

I can learn from my fears

I've been experiencing fears since the death of my loved one. I'm afraid of a number of possible outcomes. My fears may be more about "what-ifs" than likely realities, but regardless, they're revealing to me what I really care about.

Anything that I'm afraid of is something that matters to me. If I'm afraid of being lonely, that means that companionship matters to me. If I'm afraid my new life will have no purpose, that means that purpose matters to me.

Whatever it is I'm afraid of belongs in my quest to reestablish meaning in my life.

·

REFLECTION
Whenever I experience a life change,
I take steps to reactivate meaning.

Love causes grief, and only love can heal grief

This may be the ultimate paradox of life. We're born to love, but when we love, we make a deal to one day grieve. And then, when we're grieving, we need love to find our way through to hope and healing.

We need self-love to help ourselves heal, of course, but we also need the love and support of others. And ultimately, we need love to find renewed meaning in life.

It always comes back to love.

•

REFLECTION
Love is the meaning of life.

I'm selfish in my grief

My grief has me focusing on my own
challenges and needs these days.
This is normal and necessary.

To everything there is a season, and this is my
season to grieve and mourn. That's what I need to
do right now. Oh, and by the way, I need you to
help me with my grief, too. Not only do I need to
indulge my grief, I need you to indulge it too.

For a while, grief is needy. That's just how it is.
Thanks for understanding. When it's your turn to
be needy, I'll be first in line to support you.

•

REFLECTION
Wherever the pain goes, that's where I go to
offer my love and support.

I don't need to fear my triggers

I know that certain things trigger my grief.
Certain places, sights, people, words, smells, songs,
and days of the year can plunge me into sharp,
sometimes blindsiding pain.

It's tempting to avoid all triggers.
It can seem better to just stay away from
anything that I know might cause a griefburst.
But if I avoid all of these things, I'm choosing to live
in fear of my normal and necessary grief.
So what if I befriend my triggers instead?

When I befriend my triggers, their terrible power
over me starts to diminish. I begin to see them as
reminders of my love instead.

•

REFLECTION
When my grief gets triggered, I know to nurture myself.

Before I can transcend, I must descend

I can't go around or above my grief. I must go through it.

And while I'm going through it, I must encounter and express it if I'm to eventually transcend it.

In grief, things usually get worse before they get better. This is normal and necessary. I'm working on accepting wherever I am on any given day.

·

REFLECTION
I find peace in allowing what is rather than thinking it should be otherwise.

Five minutes is all it takes

Grieving and mourning can only be done effectively in doses. When I get stuck in a painful grief encounter and can't seem to shake it, I remember the five-minute rule.

If I try doing something else for just five minutes, I'm likely to get unstuck. For example, if I get up and walk for five minutes, my mood will probably shift. Or if I chat with a friend for five minutes—even if we're not talking about my loss—my day will reset.

Passive interventions can also help. Watching TV for five minutes might do it. So might listening to music. But if those don't help, I'll try something more active. Just for five minutes.

·

REFLECTION

Dosing my grief and mourning invites much-needed time-outs.

I'm open to participating in a grief support group

For many grieving people, support groups are one of the best helping resources. In a group, I can connect with others experiencing similar thoughts and feelings. I'm allowed and gently encouraged to talk about the person who died and my grief as much and as often as I like.

If I'm feeling the need for more support, or if I need somewhere to talk openly and honestly about my grief, I'll look into grief support groups, online or in my community.

I need not walk alone.

•

REFLECTION

If I see myself benefiting from a support group, I will encourage myself to attend.

Writing my grief can free my grief

I might not think of myself as someone who likes to write, but if I try jotting down my thoughts and feelings—in a journal, in a letter, in a computer file—I might find it freeing.

My grief includes thoughts and feelings that are hard for me to express. Some of my grief feels too intimate or unseemly to talk about. But it's safe to write about all of it. And in writing it down, I find that it's more approachable and even OK.

Writing about my grief is a powerful tool. I might as well give it a try.

•

REFLECTION
I'm open to expressing myself in many ways, including writing.

My grief is not a problem to be solved or fixed

Grief is a normal and necessary part of love.
It *is* love, just in another form.

Grief isn't a problem. It's not an illness.
It's not bad. There's nothing wrong about it.
I don't need to fix myself. I don't need anyone else
to try to make it go away.

What I need is to befriend my grief and for
others to befriend it too. My grief is normal and
necessary. It's part of my love, and it's something
I must experience and express.

●

REFLECTION
By openly embracing and expressing
all of my feelings, I help others embrace
and express theirs as well.

In-betweenness is hard—and essential

Grief lives in liminal space. *Limina* is the Latin word for threshold, the space betwixt and between. When I'm in this limbo, I am not busily and unthinkingly going about my daily life. Neither am I living from a place of assuredness about my relationships and beliefs.

Instead, I'm unsettled. My automatic daily routine and core beliefs have been shaken, forcing me to reconsider who I am, why I'm here, and what life means.

I'm uneasy with waiting, with not doing, with in-betweenness. But that's where I am. And I need to be here for a while.

•

REFLECTION

There is value in the suspension that comes from being in liminal space.

I'm sensitive to grief

People who've experienced a staggering loss in their lives get it. People who haven't, don't.

When it comes to loss and grief, there's no substitute for personal experience. I feel awakened to the reality of profound loss, but it seems like many other people are still asleep.

I'm in the group that gets it. When I'm in need of grief conversation and support, I'll remember to reach out to others who get it. They're my people right now.

·

REFLECTION

I can use my awareness to make this world a more grief-welcoming place.

I find myself asking why

This death has me considering the meaning of human life. Why are we here? Why did this person die? Why should I get my feet out of bed in the morning?

My search for meaning is a spiritual quest. I might be questioning my faith or looking for new spiritual answers. This takes time, and I might not always find clear answers.

Reestablishing meaning and purpose in my life is what will help me live well until I, too, die.

·

REFLECTION

Whenever I have a choice in my day or in my life,
I choose based on what is most meaningful to me
and to those I love.

How do I feel?

I'm making a habit of checking in with myself. In any given moment, I ask: How am I feeling?

It's easy to go through life unaware. But when I regularly and intentionally stop my incessant thoughts and activities to notice how I'm feeling, I realize that I think and feel many things in addition to my grief.

My loss is a significant part of my life, and so are other relationships and experiences. This realization helps me integrate my loss. In each unique moment, I am present and aware.

·

REFLECTION

Taking frequent inventory of how I feel is essential to my eventual transformation.

I get to be happy again.

One grief misconception I tell myself—and my culture sometimes tells me—is that it's unseemly for me to be happy. I've experienced a major loss, and so if I'm smiling, laughing, or having a good time, I'm sometimes judged, or I judge myself, as somehow being disloyal to the person who died.

But the truth is that when I experience moments of happiness, even in the midst of my darkest grief, I'm honoring life, and I'm honoring the person who died.

Life isn't just happiness or just grief. It's always both. In fact, it's a complicated and ever-changing mixture of lots of things. So I allow myself to feel what I feel in each moment. And when happiness naturally arises, or when I intentionally seek out circumstances that make me feel happy, I enjoy it.

•

REFLECTION

I can be sad when I'm sad, and happy when I'm happy.
To experience paradoxical emotions is good for me.

Instead of apologizing, I'm thanking

As I've been grieving, I've noticed that I sometimes apologize for being open and honest about my grief. "Sorry I'm such a mess," I might say after a crying jag in front of a friend. Or, "I'm sorry I need so much help."

But I shouldn't feel sorry about my normal and necessary grief. So now I'm switching out sorries for thank-yous: "Thank you for listening to me." "Thank you for helping me." "Thank you for being there for me."

These thank-yous honor my need to mourn and be supported in my grief. They also extend gratitude to my helpers. So much better!

·

REFLECTION
I don't have to apologize for being genuine.

I may be anticipating more grief

I've experienced a loss, and I may be anticipating more loss to come.

I might be worried about someone else dying. I might be concerned about major life changes on the horizon. I might be upset about other challenges in my life or the lives of those I love.

Anticipatory grief is common. If it's part of my grief journey, I may need a little extra support in coping and actively mourning. If my grief burden is extra challenging, it's OK for me to ask for help.

•

REFLECTION

As much as possible, I live in the present and trust that I'm capable of meeting any future challenges as they arise.

My time of grief may be an opportunity to heal old wounds

As I'm feeling and actively mourning my loss, it may be bringing up older pain—especially any significant losses in my life that were never properly and thoroughly mourned.

My heart is wise. It knows that these older griefs I'm carrying need attention, too. And it figures that now is the time, because I'm being grief-aware and proactive about healthy mourning and self-care right now, anyway.

If I have past losses to mourn and they're coming up for me right now, I may need a little extra help with all the work that needs to be done. It's true that it can be a good time to mourn older unreconciled grief, as well, but maybe I should reach out to a grief counselor for some short-term support.

·

REFLECTION

Once I've befriended all my past losses, I'll know to grieve and mourn future losses as they occur.

I'm not attached to outcome

When I set my intention each day to authentically befriend my grief and actively mourn, I'm nurturing hope for healing.

But I'm not sure exactly what that healing will look like. I don't know how my self-identity will change. I can't totally predict what my search for meaning will yield. I'm not sure how I'll live and love.

Instead, I'm open to the infinite possibilities before me.

·

REFLECTION

I'm attached to people and passions, not to outcomes.

It's never too late

If I'm reading this, it's not too late.

It's not too late to befriend my current grief.
It's not even too late to go back and engage with
any old, unreconciled griefs I may be carrying.
It's not too late to learn how to mourn well so
I can go on to live and love well for the
rest of my precious days.

If I'm reading this, I still have time to
embrace my grief and heal.

•

REFLECTION
The reality is it's never too late
to grieve and mourn.

I rest my mind regularly

When I'm grieving, difficult cognitive demands can be too much for me sometimes. If I'm having trouble completing challenging tasks or making decisions, that doesn't mean something's wrong with me. It just means my brain needs a break.

My brain is kind of like a computer. Whether I'm conscious of it or not, part of my computer is constantly running in the background in an attempt to understand and process my loss. In that way, my grief is like a giant software application that takes up a massive amount of processing power.

No wonder I can't always think well.

•

REFLECTION

I'll be kind to my mind and rest it regularly.

In part, I'm powerless in grief

Just as I wasn't able to prevent or control the death of the person who died, I'm not able to prevent or control my grief.

My grief arises naturally, without my permission or planning. I embrace it as it comes.

I'm not powerless, however, in acting on my grief. I choose to actively befriend it and express it. That's where my power lies.

.

REFLECTION
I cannot control all aspects of my grief. However,
I can allow myself to actively mourn.

Grieving is a consequence of loving

Loss and grief are difficult, but on the other hand, they are symptoms of a life well lived. How so? Because the only reason I'm grieving is that I was fortunate enough to love.

Not everyone grieves—because not everyone loves. What a sad, sad way to live.

I sometimes wish I didn't have to suffer loss, but then I remember that a lossless life is a loveless life. Grief can be a steep price to pay, but still, it is worth it.

•

REFLECTION

Every life experience based on love and connection is an experience I'm fortunate to have.

How am I surviving today?

When other people ask me, "How are you doing?", it can feel like a meaningless question. They often don't want to know how I'm really doing. They just want to be polite.

But what if they were to ask me, "How are you surviving?" Well, then I'd think they might actually be offering me genuine empathy and extending an opening for me to share.

When I need to check in with my grief, I can stop what I'm doing and ask myself the same question. How am I surviving today? This simple self-query invites me to be aware of my thoughts and feelings in the moment. And after I've synced with this awareness, I can then ask myself a follow-up question: What can I do to actively mourn these thoughts and feelings today and give them momentum?

•

REFLECTION
I'm living today.

I find gratitude for even tiny steps forward

Grief is a long, arduous journey. It's also a journey that typically gets harder before it gets easier.

It can be hard to maintain the strength I need to keep going.

But I can find that strength in gratitude. When I acknowledge the good things in my days, and when I intentionally foster awareness of even the tiny steps forward I'm making, I am creating momentum toward healing.

·

REFLECTION

As much as possible, I live in a state of wonder, awe, and gratitude.

I continue to honor the person and the relationship

The person who died was such a special, irreplaceable part of my life. While the nature of our relationship has changed, I continue to honor the person they were and the relationship we had while they were still here on earth.

For instance, I can visit the grave or permanent resting place on the anniversary of the death. Or I can buy flowers, cake, a special meal, or another fitting treat on their birthday and share it with someone else in my life. I can also make a donation or give a gift. I can even throw a little party!

Continuing to mark the significance of the person's role in my life feels right. It's an ongoing ritual of love and grief, grief and love.

·

REFLECTION

While this person is irreplaceable, I can and will continue to give honor to the life they lived.

I'm always on the lookout for things to be grateful for

Gratitude is a grief balancer. It helps me find my equilibrium in this painful time.

I train my awareness on people and things to be grateful for (including my relationship with the person who died). And I express my gratitude, too, verbally and maybe in writing.

When I fill my life with gratitude, I invoke a self-fulfilling prophecy: What I pay attention to will be magnified and repeated. I reflect on moments of love and joy each day. I honor them with gratitude. When I'm grateful, I train my brain to look for the good in life, and I prepare the way for inner peace.

•

REFLECTION
I am so grateful.

Maybe it's my grief

I'm keeping in mind that my grief can show up in lots of ways. For example, if I'm irritated at people or little life circumstances, if I'm having a hard time completing necessary tasks, or if I'm behaving in ways that aren't like me, it might not seem to be about my loss—but in fact, it might be.

So when things aren't going well or I'm feeling "off" but don't know why, I can try giving some focused attention to my grief. I can work on one or more of the six needs of mourning, in doses, one day at a time.

My grief can seep into everything.
I'll be aware of that.

•

REFLECTION

When I don't feel like myself, I can ask: "Is what I'm experiencing in some way related to my grief?"

I'm on alert for cultural expectations about gender that may affect my grief

I'm aware that my culture has traditionally had many different expectations for men and women. Some of these expectations and biases may have shaped how I see myself and how I determine what's "normal" in grief for me.

But grief is not gendered. Grief is human. If I find myself struggling with an aspect of my normal and necessary grief because it seems gender inappropriate, I'll know that I may need help breaking through gender stereotypes.

·

REFLECTION

I see my grief and mourning journey not through the lens of gender but through the lens of love.

If I see or dream of the person who died, that's normal

It's common to "see" or dream about a loved one who has died. I might glimpse someone in a passing car who looks like my loved one. I might even see my loved one or feel their unseen presence in my home. And when I dream of them, it can feel so real.

Maybe my mind and heart are searching so desperately for my loved one that they invite these images. Or maybe there is a spirit world that allows my loved one to visit me in some form.

Many grievers find comfort in these experiences. If I feel comforted by them, I can welcome them and tell friends about them as well.

·

REFLECTION

I know that my time in human form is but a blink in eternity, and I know the universe holds many more miracles than we can comprehend.

Thankfulness grows the good

Cultivating an attitude of gratitude is helping me weather my grief.

I'm thinking and feeling so many hurtful things every day. This is normal and natural, but I need respite from my pain, and I need hope, too. One reliable place to find both respite and hope is in gratitude.

What am I thankful for? When I intentionally ask myself this question and take the time to answer it, I come up with so many reasons to continue to live and love well. Being thankful not only recognizes the good in my life, it grows it. Because when I move thankfully through my days, that energy strengthens my relationships with others, helps me make better decisions, and encourages me to practice good self-care.

·

REFLECTION
Thinking just one thankful thought lifts my spirits.

Griefbursts are normal, and I'll have them forever

Even long after I've reconciled my grief, I will probably experience sudden, strong waves of grief from time to time. These are called griefbursts, and they're normal.

Griefbursts can seem to come out of nowhere but are often triggered by a smell, a place, a song, or a memory. They can often be painful, yet at the same time comforting

I like to think that griefbursts are there to remind me of the deep love I still feel for the person who died.

·

REFLECTION

When I experience a griefburst, I welcome it, stop what I'm doing, spend time with it, and feel grateful for the reminder it brings me.

I am truly doing well with my grief

Society tends to believe that "doing well" in grief means being "strong" and "in control." But the truth is that doing well with my grief actually requires vulnerability and honest encounters with all of my thoughts and feelings.

When I embrace my pain, I'm doing well with my grief. When I express what I really and truly think and feel, I'm doing well with my grief.

·

REFLECTION

Ironically, it is in embracing my pain
that I'm "doing well" in my grief.

Closure is a misconception

People tell me I should be finding "closure" in my grief, but that's a misconception. My love and grief will never end. I will never fully close the door on my loss.

Yet I'm working toward integrating my loss into my ongoing life. This will help me arrive at some degree of peace over what has happened. The days of intense and constant turmoil can slowly be replaced by acceptance and days of love, hope, and joy.

●

REFLECTION
I accept that life is constant change.

I breathe and take it slowly

Inhale slowly. Exhale slowly. Repeat.

Sometimes that's the only thing I can do to make it through a challenging grief moment or day.

And you know what? When that's all I can do, that's enough.

•

Mindful attention to my breath
can always help re-center me.

It's my time to lean

I need to lean on others for support right now.
No ifs, ands, or buts about it.

If in the past I've been reluctant to turn to others
for help, it's time for me to rethink my biases. Stoic
"strength" is actually a weakness. Vulnerability is
what's genuine, connecting, and life-affirming.

In fact, one of the miracles of vulnerability is that it
opens my life not only to healing but to more joy.
So even if it's scary or uncomfortable for me, I'm
going to do some leaning today. Here I go.

•

REFLECTION

If we all held each other up, what a world this would be.

I hold onto whatever helps me through

Some days I'm desperate for an idea, belief, or plan
to hang onto. I grasp for something—anything—
that will help me survive that day.
I need a life preserver to hold onto that will give
me hope that I can and will survive this and
that all will eventually be well.

Whatever I find to hold onto that works for me in
those moments is a good and legitimate thing.

Sometimes others will judge these ideas, beliefs,
or plans as ill-conceived, silly, or fake.
But it doesn't matter what they think.

·

REFLECTION
What matters is that I'm staying afloat.

I FEEL my feelings

What does it mean to embrace my grief? It means to FEEL—Freely Experience Emotion with Love.

First, I allow my emotions to flow over and through me, no matter what they are. I allow them to run freely in and around me.

Second, I experience the emotions. I welcome them, and I sit with them. I give them the time and space they need.

And third, I love them. My grief feelings are, after all, part of my love. I love them without condition or judgment.

·

REFLECTION

I FEEL. I attend to my emotions as they arise in each moment while remaining stable and calm at my core.

Over time, I'm seeing the forest for the trees

In the beginning of my grief, my loss was a giant sequoia rising out of the ground right in front of me. It was all I could see. The rest of the world was carrying on beyond and all around the sequoia, of course, but I couldn't see the forest for the tree.

This all-consuming, single focus of loss is normal and necessary, especially in the early weeks and months. But lately, I'm been finding a little more separation between me and that sequoia. Over time and through active mourning, I'm creating a little more space in my life for other people, activities, and experiences. That sequoia will always be a giant in my life, but it won't always be the only thing.

•

REFLECTION

I'm starting to gain more perspective.
I'm starting to see the forest for the trees.

I grieve the loss of those I love as well as those I like, dislike, hate, or feel ambivalent about

Grief exists on a continuum. We think of it in association with the deaths of those we love, but in truth, it arises when anyone we have feelings of any kind for dies.

Ongoing relationship feelings create attachments, and the severing of attachments is what really creates grief. If a family member I had a challenging relationship with dies, for example, I'm likely to feel grief.

And after a death, ambivalent relationships often give rise to particularly complicated grief. I also need to grieve what I longed for but never was. If I'm grieving the loss of a relationship that wasn't all about love, that's normal.

•

REFLECTION

I must remember that relationships are built on
a complex and fluid mixture of feelings.

When I'm courageous, I give myself credit

Grief takes so much courage. It's so hard to put my feet on the floor each morning. It takes courage just to get up, get going, and face the day.

And now I'm being told I need to not only acknowledge my grief, I need to embrace it. And even more than that, I need to express it outside of myself, day in and day out.

Grief and mourning are hard work. When I muster the courage to take even a small step, I acknowledge my effort, and I give myself credit.

•

REFLECTION
The secret of being able to actively mourn is to have the courage to do so.

When I'm feeling stressed, I can pivot to gratitude

The ongoing stress of grief may be normal, but it can also make me unwell physically, emotionally, and spiritually. So when I'm feeling this unwellness, I can purposefully pivot to gratitude.

I may be grateful for the beauty of nature outside my window, for my dog sleeping at my feet, or for the friend I met for lunch. I then express that gratitude. I can say a prayer of thanks for this spectacular world. I can have a chat with my dog. I can write a note to my friend. Or I can make an entry in my gratitude journal.

It's almost impossible to feel gratitude and stress at the same time.

·

REFLECTION

Stress comes from ego. Peace comes from essence.

I don't overdo it

When people are recovering from a physical injury or surgery, they're told to take it slow and easy. They're supposed to proactively work their way back toward health—one careful bit at a time.

That's how I'm treating my grief wound, too. I'm taking it slow and easy. I'm proactively mourning my way toward healing, but I'm doing it one careful dose at a time.

I'm not overdoing it. There are no rewards for speed. But if I ever feel especially bruised and battered, I'm sure to give myself some extra pampering, support, and downtime. This helps me return to my healing journey refreshed and ready to encounter each new day again.

·

REFLECTION
I appreciate the slow and the gentle.

I speak the name

Talking about the person who died is one way
I keep their memory alive.

Sometimes people are afraid to bring up the
person who died or to speak their name. So I
speak it freely and often. This helps other people
know that they can talk about them too.

Just because this precious person is gone from the
earth doesn't mean their life doesn't continue to
resonate here on earth. It does. And the
more I speak the name, the more those
resonances get amplified.

·

REFLECTION

I not only speak their names, but I find ways to
regularly honor the lives of the precious people
who have gone before me.

I must make friends with the darkness before I can enter the light

Grief is a dark time in my life. It's naturally and necessarily dark. The darkness is painful and scary, but it's not bad. It is the reality of my love right now. I must befriend the darkness.

When I allow myself to sit in the blackness without trying to fight it, deny it, or run away from it, I find that it has something to teach me.

Befriending pain is hard. It's true that it's easier to avoid, repress, or deny the pain than it is to embrace it, but it's in befriending it that I learn from it and unlock my capacity to be transformed by it.

·

REFLECTION

I attend, befriend, and surrender to my dark emotions.

I'm searching for meaning, and it takes time to find it

The fifth need of mourning is to search for meaning. It's something I naturally do when I wonder "Why?" and "How?" questions.

While searching for meaning is instinctual and immediate, I'm seeing that finding meaning takes time. First come the shock, numbness, and searing pain. The heightened emotions. The acknowledging of the reality and the embracing of the hurt. Only over many months and possibly years and through active, ongoing mourning do I begin to explore ever-deeper meaning questions and try on possible answers.

I may never find satisfactory answers to all these questions. But I can find meaning in the search and in the eventual decisions I make about living on.

●

REFLECTION

In small, everyday moments there is much meaning.

It's OK for me to feel happiness

Grieving people are whole human beings, just like everyone else. We may often be sad, anxious, or irritated, but we can also laugh, have fun, and experience joy.

When I find myself inside moments of laughter or happiness, it doesn't mean I'm not grieving. It doesn't mean I don't still deeply miss and love the person who died. It just means the loss is not my totality, just like the relationship I had with the person who died was not my totality. I have independent thoughts, feelings, and interests.

I might also laugh and feel happiness sometimes when I remember the person who died. This is more than OK—this is grace and healing.

•

REFLECTION

I have gratitude for every moment.

Pain is part of life

Loss and pain are a normal part of our human experience. Because we have the capacity to form attachments, we come to grief in the face of loss.

Yes, if we are able to love (and not everyone can), we come to know about the hurt that is grief.

We can't change that. But what we can change is how we as a culture respond to grief. We can get better—*a lot better*—at supporting people who are grieving.

As I learn about grief and what true grief support looks like, I'm helping support others. And in doing so, I'm working to change our cultural dysfunction around grief.

·

REFLECTION

I commit myself to helping others in grief understand the role of hurt, pain, and suffering in healing.

There's nothing wrong with me

Grief is normal and necessary. When I'm grieving, there is nothing "wrong" with me. If the circumstances of my loss were particularly challenging, my grief may be complicated—but still, there is nothing wrong with me.

If love is not a disease (which of course it is not!), then grief is not a disease, either. I'm simply experiencing the thoughts and feelings that arise naturally after a significant loss.

·

REFLECTION

My capacity to love requires the necessity to mourn.

I'm learning to recognize grief misconceptions and instead choose the truth

Our grief-avoiding culture tends to spread misconceptions about grief. These misconceptions are harmful to me and to all grievers.

Grief misconceptions deny my right to hurt and to authentically and openly express my natural, necessary grief.

Here are some truths: Grief isn't bad. Grief doesn't progress in predictable, orderly stages. I will never "get over" my grief.

•

REFLECTION

When I hear someone unknowingly share a grief misconception, I gently guide them toward the truth.

I remember the rule of thirds

When it comes to supporting me in my grief, some people in my life are helpful, some are neutral, and some are harmful. On average, mourners find that they have about a third of each group in their life.

There's a spectrum of empathy and emotional intelligence. Some people are good at empathy and listening. Those are my helpers. I'm remembering to turn to those people first when I want to talk about my grief or share memories.

My neutral people might still be good companions when I want to socialize or spend time with others. But the people who try to shame me for my grief or tell me what I should or shouldn't be doing— those people I'll avoid for the time being.

•

REFLECTION

I accept people as they are without judgment. I have empathy for the fact that they have each been uniquely shaped by the mentors and circumstances in their lives.

I'm on the lookout for signs of reconciliation

I'll know that I'm moving toward reconciling my grief when it starts to feel like an integral part of my life story. I will feel that my relationship with the person who died is changing from one of presence to one of memory (and perhaps one of hoped-for eventual reunion).

I find momentum toward reconciliation in active mourning. The more I engage with my grief and actively mourn over time, the more I will feel the pain of my grief softening. The intensity will fade. Hope for my continued life will emerge as I'm able to make commitments to the future.

·

REFLECTION

Reconciling myself to life's changes comes more and more naturally to me.

I find ways to remember and honor on special days

When special days like birthdays, anniversaries, and holidays come around, I really feel and grieve my loved one's absence. It's so hard.

To engage with my grief on those days, I'm finding new ways to keep my loved one close. I can visit the final resting place, write and read a letter aloud, light a candle, gather friends and family together to share stories, volunteer for a cause that was meaningful to my loved one, or carry out a random act of kindness.

My new rituals of remembrance
and honor incorporate my forever grief
and love into my ongoing life.

•

REFLECTION

I will slow down on special days and give
honor to those who have gone before me.

"What do you want?"
I ask myself

Before this loss turned my life upside-down,
I was more likely to move unthinkingly through
my days. I didn't often stop to ask myself if I was
living the life I wanted to be living.

But my grief has stopped me in my tracks.
It has me asking lots of questions about who
I really am and what I really care about.

"What do you really want?" I ask myself.
And I listen hard and wait for my heart to speak.

•

REFLECTION

I am learning to distinguish the voice of my ego
from the voice of my heart. I will ignore the
former and tune in to the latter.

Sometimes I experience borrowed tears

Sometimes I'm brought to tears by something that has little or no apparent connection to my grief and loss.

I might find myself crying when I watch a movie or commercial. Or I might see a random human interaction and feel the prick of tears.

I'm crying because my heart and soul are hurting and my emotions are tender. Because my heart is wounded right now, anything that touches it even slightly can hurt. This is normal and will pass as my heart is healed.

·

REFLECTION

I know that vulnerability is a strength,
and I welcome being touched by life.

It's no wonder if I worry

Anxiety and fear are normal parts of grief.
This death has caused a major disruption,
knocking lots of things out of kilter.
It's no wonder if I feel anxious.

As a result of the death, my everyday life
may be changing in significant ways. Or my hopes
and dreams for the future may be changing.
Or I might be worried about more
unwanted losses and changes.

All the uncertainty and change has me worrying.
But when I talk to trusted listeners about my
fears, they begin to subside.
That's the magic of mourning.

·

REFLECTION
When I give attention to my fears,
they begin to soften.

I learned about grief and mourning as a child

When I was growing up, I saw how my parents and other important grown-ups in my life handled grief and loss. I know if they were open and honest or closed and silent. I know if grief and mourning were considered normal and necessary or shameful and weak.

Whatever I learned as child I bring to my grief journey now. I do have the power to unlearn any harmful misconceptions, however. The commitment and ongoing effort this takes is worth it.

I learned about grief and mourning as a child, and I am learning anew as an adult.

•

REFLECTION

I proactively teach the children in my life that grief is normal and necessary, and that it's important to mourn openly and honestly.

It's healthy to let others help me

I can't heal alone—nor should I try to. I need support now, and I'll need it for a long time to come.

I need to talk about my grief, and I need others to listen. I need hugs and human touch. I need company when I'm feeling lonely. I might need practical help, too, with life tasks.

Mourning is the shared social response to loss. I need to mourn in order to heal…so I need a social group to share with.

·

REFLECTION

I will allow myself to seek and accept the support I need and deserve.

I grieve, and I celebrate

Even as I'm actively grieving and mourning, I can celebrate my life. I'm privileged to be alive, and if I open myself to this awareness, I notice that each day presents me with treasures and wonders.

Grief is teaching me that life is precious. It's teaching me the importance of living as much and as well as I can in the present moment.

Today I will notice, and I will celebrate.

•

REFLECTION

I celebrate even my grief, because I deeply understand that it is part of my love.

An imperfect life can still be a wonderful life

Great loss is proof that life is imperfect. But at the same time, it's also proof that life is wonderful.

Come again?

Great loss means that I've been privileged to experience great love. And that's the most wonderful thing of all. This truth doesn't take away my need to grieve and mourn deeply. But when I'm ready, it does offer me good perspective.

•

REFLECTION

Imperfection is more perfect than perfection.

I invite peace into my soul

In grief, peace comes with fully accepting
and surrendering to the reality of what happened.
It takes time and active mourning to reconcile
myself to this reality and for peace to
begin to replace the normal disbelief,
protest, and yearning.

As I move toward surrender, I can, with intention,
invite peace into my soul. I can sit in stillness
(especially in the healing environment of nature)
and inhale peace while exhaling resistance.

Whenever I feel myself resisting, I can stop to
notice the tightness of resistance and welcome the
expansiveness and comfort of peace instead.

·

REFLECTION
As I grieve and mourn, I consciously
invite peace into my life.

I don't need to think ten steps ahead

As I journey through the wilderness of my grief,
I only need to think about the next step.

If I try to project too far ahead, I sometimes get
discouraged. Or I wobble on the step I'm taking
right now because my attention is elsewhere.

If I focus on this step as I'm taking it, and then the
next step as I'm taking that one, and so on,
I'll be fine in the long run.

•

REFLECTION
What do you mean, ten steps ahead?
There is only this step.

There is hope and help online

When I'm not getting all the support
I need from friends and family face-to-face,
I can seek out support online.

I can read up on the basic principles of grief and
mourning. I can join a grief message board or
online support group. I can share thoughts and
receive support in return on social media.

While not everything to be found online is
accurate or healthy, I'll know I've found good
support when it makes me feel seen,
understood, and empathized with.

•

REFLECTION
I can be discerning about any
potential use of online grief resources.

It's all about my people

My relationship with a special person is what set my eventual grief in motion. And it's my remaining special people (including those I have yet to meet) who will help me through my grief and back to love and meaning.

I think I'll put down this book and reach out to one of my special people in some way right this very moment. That's where the healing happens.

•

REFLECTION

When in doubt, I reach out.

Today is a day for healing

Today is a day to engage with my grief.

Today is a day to actively mourn.

Today is a day to move toward healing.

·

Today is a gift.

I'm entering a new year as a new me

I'm not the same person I was before my loss. So much has changed.

As I work on developing my new self-identity, I realize that I've never been static. Throughout my life, I've constantly changed and grown. So while I'm entering this new year as a new me, I know that the same thing will be true the following year and the one after that.

Change is hard, but it's also kind of a relief to know that I still have time to pursue my goals, follow my dreams, and be the me I would like to be. What a gift it is to still have time.

•

REFLECTION
I don't just change—I evolve.

A Final Word

If you've spent the past twelve months with this book as your daily companion, you're a different person than you were a year ago. You're still grieving, but you've followed the ten touchstones, you've actively engaged with the six needs of mourning, and your life and your grief have changed.

Perhaps the pain has subsided a bit, and the love behind it has stepped forward a bit more. Maybe you're sleeping better. Maybe you've discovered some parts of yourself you'd forgotten about or didn't know were there. Perhaps you're finding glimmers of new meaning in certain practices, activities, and relationships.

No matter how your grief may have changed in the last year, I want to congratulate you for authentically engaging with and expressing it. Your love is not only deep and true, it is courageous.

You may want to reread this book in the coming year. You'll find that as you recommit to the ideas it contains, they will speak to you in new and different ways. Or if you've found this book helpful, you may want to pass it along to someone else who is grieving.

Thank you for letting me be a small part of your healing. One final invitation, please consider writing me at drwolfelt@centerforloss.com to let me know how your year of understanding your grief has unfolded.

I hope we meet one day.

ALSO BY ALAN WOLFELT

Grief One Day at a Time: 365 Meditations to Help You Heal After Loss

After someone you love dies, each day can be a struggle. But each day, you can also find comfort and understanding in this daily companion. With one brief entry for every day of the calendar year, this little book offers small, one-day-at-a-time doses of guidance and healing. Each entry includes an inspiring or soothing quote followed by a short discussion of the day's theme.

How do you get through the loss of a loved one? One day at a time. This compassionate gem of a book will accompany you.

"Each day I look forward to reading a new page...I can't imagine dealing with my sorrow without [this] book."
— A reader

ISBN 978-1-61722-238-2 • 384 pages • softcover • $14.95

All Dr. Wolfelt's publications can be ordered by mail from:
Companion Press, 3735 Broken Bow Road, Fort Collins, CO 80526
(970) 226-6050 • www.centerforloss.com

ALSO BY ALAN WOLFELT

One Mindful Day at a Time: 365 Meditations for Living in the Now

For most of us, life is way too hectic. We feel scattered and distracted. We're busy rushing from one required activity to the next, and when we have a few moments of downtime, we're often glued to our electronics. Is this what life is really all about?

Learn to slow down and live more mindfully with this daily companion. In one brief entry for each day of the calendar year, counselor Dr. Alan Wolfelt offers small, day-at-a-time doses of wisdom and practical guidance.

In just a few minutes a day, this little gem of a book will teach you to live every moment from a place of peace, purpose, and gratitude. Living in the now is a habit you can cultivate. Let's get started.

ISBN: 978-1-61722-263-4 • 384 pages • softcover • $14.95

All Dr. Wolfelt's publications can be ordered by mail from:
Companion Press, 3735 Broken Bow Road, Fort Collins, CO 80526
(970) 226-6050 • www.centerforloss.com